Manju Malhi has inspired [...] pproach to cooking Indian food at home, with TV shows in Asia as well as the UK. In her cuisine, she draws on her heritage and combines it with the realities of Western life to come up with delicious dishes using good ingredients. Manju grew up surrounded by Indian culture and traditions and several years of her childhood were spent in India. Spices run through her veins and their beneficial properties play an important part in her approach to good food and healthy living. Manju Malhi lives in London, where she teaches people of all ages – from eight to eighty – how to cook healthily and in return they laugh at her jokes.

Other titles

Everyday Healthy Indian Cookery

Manju Malhi

....

A How To Book

ROBINSON

First published in Great Britain in 2017 by Robinson

10 9 8 7 6 5 4 3 2 1

A CIP catalogue record for this book is available from the British Library.

ISBN: 978-1-47213-962-7

Typeset by Basement Press, Glaisdale
Printed and bound in Great Britain by Clays Ltd, St Ives plc

Papers used by Robinson are from well-managed forests and other responsible sources.

MIX
Paper from
responsible sources
FSC® C104740

Robinson
An imprint of
Little, Brown Book Group
Carmelite House
50 Victoria Embankment
London EC4Y 0DZ

An Hachette UK Company
www.hachette.co.uk

www.littlebrown.co.uk

Contents

How to use spices as part of a healthy, balanced diet

Who doesn't enjoy a good curry? A trip to the local Indian restaurant has become a regular part of modern British life. But like many eating-out experiences, Indian food has developed something of a reputation for being calorie-laden. However, in the right hands, Indian cuisine can be among the healthiest in the world. Its herbs and spices are like an edible apothecary, offering all manner of benefits to the body.

Spices are strongly flavoured or aromatic parts of plants, and are used in small quantities in food as a flavouring or preservative. In Indian cooking, spices are used fresh or dried, whole, broken, crushed or ground to a powder. Besides their culinary uses, spices have also been used medicinally since ancient times. Not only are spices the key to authentic Indian food, they are also central to the traditional system of medicine known as Ayurveda. Many spices and herbs are used for their healing properties, including black pepper, cardamom, cinnamon, cloves, cumin, fenugreek, ginger, nutmeg, paprika, saffron, turmeric and even vanilla.

Early Indians ate food that was easily available from nature: fruits and berries, meat and fish were the main food items of the country's nomadic inhabitants. When people began to settle in the fertile river valleys they were able to cultivate crops such as cereals and pulses, and to domesticate animals. Rice, lentils, vegetables and meat were all flavoured with a few locally grown spices. As civilisation developed, the wealthy were able to access spices from further afield, and India became known for its richly spiced foods.

There is a well-known ancient Hindu Sanskrit saying that the 'guest is god' when entering an Indian household. And that is reflected in the ancient traditions of serving food. Fruits and sweets made from milk were offered to guests as part of the ritual. This enormous generosity with food thrives in many Asian households around the world. Food is a medium for the expression of love and relationships. Eating for Indians is without doubt an art form that has been cultivated over the centuries, and spices are the stars.

In India today, 'rich' foods have come to mean salty, creamy and oily foods, rather than richly spiced dishes. Increased urbanisation, less physical activity and the introduction of processed foods has led to a rise in diet-related diseases such as diabetes, obesity, high blood pressure and heart disease in what is an increasingly sedentary lifestyle. But there is a middle ground, where a balanced diet results in a healthier lifestyle.

This cookbook shows you how easy it is to eat healthily with Indian cuisine – whether you're new to Indian cooking or simply want to surprise your guests with something spicy and different. Many of the recipes highlight the health-promoting properties of spices. Making healthier Indian home-cooked meals doesn't mean you have to sacrifice flavour. Seasoning your dishes with spices will enable you to use less of other, less healthy, ingredients such as salt, added sugars and saturated fat.

There is an Indian tradition of adding salt to food because it is thought to balance the flavours of spices. Salt is often not measured but is generously scattered into dishes. However, eating too much salt has been linked to high blood pressure and increased risk of stroke. Salt is the common term for sodium chloride; it's the sodium part of the compound which is considered to be harmful if taken in excess. Rock salt, mineral salt, sea salt, pink salt and coarse salt may include other minerals, but if they contain sodium then that is something to be

Cooking fats and oils

In this book I use various oils, including olive, sunflower and coconut, as well as butter and ghee. In many recipes these are interchangeable, although butter and ghee add a somewhat richer flavour. All fats and oils are high in calories and should be used in moderation. Avoid deep-fried foods, not only because of their high fat content, but also because the high temperature can damage the molecular structure of the fat, making it hazardous to health.

Ghee is a type of clarified butter: it is made by melting butter and removing the milk solids and impurities. It has a higher smoking point than other oils, which makes it a good choice for frying. However, vegetable ghee (used in some Indian restaurants) may contain trans fats, which are detrimental to health and have been found to increase the risk of heart disease.

wary of. The recommended intake for adults is no more than 6g of salt per day – the equivalent of just over a teaspoon. However, as salt is present in many of our everyday and shop-bought foods it can be difficult to control how much we eat, other than in what we cook from scratch. The good news is that as almost every Indian dish uses spice for flavour, there is no need to add much salt. For most dishes that serve four people I have suggested a quarter teaspoon of salt as an optional addition. I recommend investing in a set of measuring spoons rather than liberally sprinkling salt straight into the pot. But I have found that by gradually reducing the amount of salt I use, my palate has adjusted to appreciating the flavours of spices much more.

Indian cuisine is packed with flavour and the liberal use of fresh vegetables, pulses (legumes), yogurt, rice and other grains makes it inherently healthy as well. Vegetables and pulses, in particular, are high in dietary fibre, which keeps you feeling full for longer, and this should help you to cut down on less healthy snacks and sweets.

Spices form the backbone of Indian cooking, and although the list of spices used to prepare some recipes may look intimidating, they provide alluring layers of flavours in a matter of minutes. Whether you're preparing a quick curry for an easy weeknight meal or a medley of dishes for an Indian-themed dinner party, you'll find these recipes to be simple, healthy, flavourful and delicious. Preparing food in a calm, collected and chilled way makes the whole experience of cooking and eating an enjoyable affair. I hope you'll be able to spend some time with me as your guide to achieving mouthwatering dishes in minutes.

CHAPTER 1

Spice Blends

Indian food without spices is like a summer without sunshine. While some of the dishes in this book focus on just one or two spices, others blend together a range of flavours: this chapter includes some of the most popular spice blends. Once you get to know these amazing flavours, you'll find it easy to cut down on salt in your cooking. Try reducing your salt intake gradually over three weeks; your taste buds will accept the change and will become more sensitive to increased salt levels. Spice blends can replace excess salt and add depth of flavour to your dishes.

The spice blends in this chapter are easy to prepare. You can make them in advance and store them in airtight containers away from sunlight, heat and moisture for up to six months.

Chaat Masala Spice Blend

Chaat is a term that describes a range of hot and tangy snacks. Chaat masala is a mixture of spices whose combination creates this zingy flavour. Although this blend is sometimes used in cooking in northern India, it's more often sprinkled over a salad or cooked vegetable dish as a garnish.

PREPARATION TIME: 5 MINUTES
COOKING TIME: 1 MINUTE
MAKES 6 TABLESPOONS

3 tbsp cumin seeds
1 tbsp coriander seeds
1½ tsp fennel seeds
4 tbsp mango powder (amchur)
3 tbsp powdered black salt
1½ tsp carom (ajwain, ajowan) seeds
1½ tsp freshly ground black pepper
¼ tsp asafoetida
1½ tsp ginger powder
1 tsp dried powdered mint

1 Heat a flat griddle or frying pan on a medium heat. When hot, add the cumin, coriander and fennel seeds and toast until the seeds begin to turn a little darker and start to release their aromas. Stir often while toasting, to prevent the seeds from burning. Tip the toasted seeds on to a plate and leave to cool.
2 When they're completely cold, put the seeds into a spice mill, coffee grinder or food processor. Add all the other ingredients and grind to a fine powder. Store in an airtight container away from sunlight.

Chicken Masala Spice Blend

This spice blend works well with poultry dishes and can also be used for a delicious mixed vegetable curry.

PREPARATION TIME: 5 MINUTES
COOKING TIME: 1 MINUTE
MAKES APPROXIMATELY 5 TABLESPOONS

8–10 peppercorns
1 tsp cumin seeds
1 tbsp fennel seeds
6 cloves
4 green cardamoms
2 black cardamoms
2.5cm piece of cinnamon stick or cassia bark
2 star anise
¼ tsp fenugreek seeds (optional)
1 tbsp ground coriander
½ tsp turmeric
¼ tsp grated nutmeg
1–2 tsp chilli powder

1 Heat a frying pan on a medium heat and add all the whole spices: the peppercorns, cumin seeds, fennel seeds, cloves, green and black cardamoms, cinnamon or cassia, star anise and fenugreek seeds, if using. Stir for 30 seconds to a minute until the spices release their aromas.
2 Remove the pan from the heat and then add the ground coriander, turmeric, nutmeg and chilli powder and stir.
3 Grind the mixture to a fine powder in a spice mill, coffee grinder or a pestle and mortar. Store in an airtight container away from sunlight.

East Indian Five-Spice Blend – Panch Phoran

The spice mix known as *panch phoran* (literally, 'five spices') is a speciality of Bengali cuisine. It generally consists of fenugreek seeds, cumin seeds, mustard seeds, nigella seeds and fennel seeds in equal quantities. However, some cooks reduce the amount of fenugreek seeds as these may impart a bitter taste. Nigella seeds (known as kalonji, and sometimes called black onion seeds) are thought to reduce cholesterol levels. Panch phoran gives a distinctive flavour to pulse and vegetable dishes. To use it, the whole seeds are fried in a little hot oil (a process known as tempering) before other ingredients are added.

PREPARATION TIME: 2 MINUTES
MAKES APPROXIMATELY 5 TEASPOONS

½ tsp fenugreek seeds
1 tsp cumin seeds
1 tsp brown mustard seeds
1 tsp nigella seeds
1 tsp fennel seeds

1 Mix the seeds together and store in an airtight container away from sunlight.
2 Use the panch phoran blend as whole seeds, or grind to a powder just before you need it. In a recipe to serve 4 people you will need about 1 teaspoon of panch phoran.

Garam Masala – Hot Spice Blend

One of the best-known of India's spice blends, garam masala literally means 'a mixture of hot spices'. It is often added at the end of the cooking time rather than at the beginning and is an integral part of most curry dishes from northern India.

PREPARATION TIME: 5 MINUTES
COOKING TIME: 2 MINUTES
MAKES APPROXIMATELY 2 TABLESPOONS

4 x 5cm pieces of cinnamon stick or cassia bark
12 bay leaves
5 black cardamoms
20 green cardamoms
4–5 pieces of mace
1 tsp fennel seeds
1 tsp cloves
1 tsp black peppercorns

1   Heat a frying pan on a medium to low heat until you can feel the heat rising. Add the cinnamon or cassia, bay leaves and black and green cardamoms and roast for 30 seconds, shaking the pan.
2   Add the mace, fennel seeds, cloves and peppercorns and continue roasting, shaking the pan, for about 1 minute more, or until you can smell the aroma of the spices. Watch carefully so they do not burn.
3   Tip the spices on to a plate and leave to cool.
4   When they're completely cold, transfer the spices to a spice mill or coffee grinder and grind to a fine powder. Store in an airtight container away from sunlight.

Curry Powder Spice Blend

Curry powder generally includes chilli, turmeric, coriander and cumin among other spices and can often be used as a 'go to' spice blend. You can use this blend in the Vegetable Chop recipe (page 34) and Egg Curry (page 42).

PREPARATION TIME: 5 MINUTES
COOKING TIME: 2 MINUTES

½ tsp cumin seeds
½ tsp fennel seeds
½ tsp coriander seeds
6 cloves
4 green cardamoms
2.5cm piece of cinnamon stick or cassia bark
10 black peppercorns
2 dried red chillies
2 bay leaves
½ tsp turmeric

1   Heat a frying pan on a medium heat and add all the spices except the turmeric. Toast them for a couple of minutes, shaking the pan from time to time to prevent them burning, until they begin to release their aromas.
2   Tip the spices on to a plate and leave to cool.
3   When they are completely cold, transfer them, along with the turmeric, to a spice mill or a coffee grinder and grind to a medium to fine powder. Store in an airtight container away from sunlight.

Chana Masala Spice Blend

This is a combination of warming spices that works well with many chickpea, lentil and pulse dishes.

PREPARATION TIME: 5 MINUTES
COOKING TIME: 1 MINUTE
MAKES APPROXIMATELY 5 TABLESPOONS

3 tbsp coriander seeds
3 dried red chillies
2 tsp fennel seeds
8–10 cloves
2 black cardamoms
2 tbsp cumin seeds
1 cinnamon stick
2 star anise
1 tsp black peppercorns
a small piece of mace (optional)
2 tsp dried pomegranate seeds or mango powder (amchur)

1 Heat a frying pan on a medium heat and add all the spices, except the pomegranate seeds or mango powder. Toast for a minute until you can smell the aroma of the spices.
2 Leave to cool for a few minutes.
3 Add the pomegranate seeds or mango powder, then transfer to a spice mill or coffee grinder and grind to a medium to fine powder. Store in an airtight container away from sunlight.

Kolhapuri Spice Blend

Kolhapur is a district in the western Indian state of Maharashtra. The food of the region is spicy and hot, with a special spice blend that is used predominantly in meat dishes.

PREPARATION TIME: 5 MINUTES
COOKING TIME: 2 MINUTES
MAKES APPROXIMATELY 2 TABLESPOONS

1 tsp coriander seeds
1 tsp cumin seeds
¼ tsp brown mustard seeds
1 tsp black peppercorns
5–6 cloves
¼ tsp fenugreek seeds
¼ tsp fennel seeds
pinch of poppy seeds (optional)
1 bay leaf (optional)
¼ tsp chilli powder
pinch of grated nutmeg (optional)

1   Heat a frying pan on a medium heat and add all the spices except for the chilli powder and nutmeg, if using. Toast for a couple of minutes, shaking the pan and making sure they don't burn.
2   Tip the spices on to a plate and leave to cool.
3   Transfer to a spice mill or coffee grinder, along with the chilli powder and nutmeg, and grind to a medium to fine powder. Store in an airtight container away from sunlight.

Northern Indian Spice Blend

This recipe uses cashew nuts, which contain a high proportion of monounsaturated fats – which can help to reduce cholesterol – as well as many nutritious minerals, such as magnesium and zinc. I've also used mace, the covering around the nutmeg seed, for an additional flavour dimension.

PREPARATION TIME: 5 MINUTES
COOKING TIME: 2 MINUTES
MAKES ABOUT 5 TEASPOONS

8–10 unsalted cashew nuts
3 green cardamoms
1 bay leaf
2–3 black peppercorns
2–3 cloves
2.5cm piece of cinnamon stick or cassia bark
1 piece of mace (optional)

1 Heat a frying pan on a medium heat, add all the ingredients and stir for 30 seconds to a minute until aromatic.
2 Tip the mixture on to a plate and leave to cool.
3 Transfer to a spice mill, coffee grinder or a pestle and mortar and grind to a fine powder. Store in an airtight container away from sunlight.

Pav Bhaji Masala Spice Blend

Star anise, or *chakra phool* as it is known in Hindi, has antibacterial properties and can help to treat yeast infections such as candida. Pav bhaji masala is a spice blend used in Mumbai to create the street snack known as Pav Bhaji (page 28): mashed spiced vegetables on toasted bread buns.

PREPARATION TIME: 10 MINUTES
COOKING TIME: 2 MINUTES
MAKES ABOUT 6 TABLESPOONS

2 tbsp coriander seeds
1 tbsp cumin seeds
4 dried red chillies
2 bay leaves
¼ tsp black peppercorns
6 cloves
1 black cardamom
seeds from 2 green cardamoms
2 x 2cm pieces of cinnamon stick or cassia bark
2 star anise
1 tsp fennel seeds
1 tbsp mango powder (amchur)
1 heaped tsp ginger powder
¼ tsp asafoetida
1 tsp turmeric

1 Heat a frying pan on a medium heat and add all the whole spices: the coriander and cumin seeds, red chillies, bay leaves, peppercorns, cloves, black cardamom, cardamom seeds, cinnamon or cassia, star anise and fennel seeds. Stir for 30 seconds to a minute until the spices release their aromas.

2 Remove the pan from the heat and then add the mango powder, ginger, asafoetida and turmeric and mix well.

3 Grind the mixture to a fine powder in a spice mill, coffee grinder or a pestle and mortar. Store in an airtight container away from sunlight.

Indian Chicken Stock

Use this to make soups and curry sauces for poultry dishes. What's more, if you're not vegetarian, this stock can also add extra flavour and lift your lentil and vegetable dishes.

PREPARATION TIME: 5 MINUTES
COOKING TIME: 35 MINUTES
MAKES APPROXIMATELY 500ML

700g chicken pieces, with bones
4 cloves
2cm piece of cinnamon stick
2 garlic cloves, peeled
4 black peppercorns
1 tsp cumin seeds

1 Place the chicken pieces in a large saucepan and add 1 litre of cold water. Add the cloves, cinnamon, garlic, peppercorns and cumin seeds. Bring to the boil, cover and simmer for 30 minutes.
2 Strain the stock into a bowl or large jug and leave it to cool.
3 Cover and store in the fridge for up to a week. Alternatively, freeze in small plastic containers for up to 3 months.

CHAPTER 2

Snacks and Light Bites

Snacking is almost a pastime in itself in many Asian households. Eating a wide range of different foods at regular intervals and in the right proportions is a healthy way of eating a balanced diet. However, if you like snacks that are high in fat, salt and sugar, that's less healthy; make sure you eat them only once in a while and in small quantities. The snacks in this chapter are slightly out of the ordinary. Many of them can also be enjoyed as light meals, with a salad or vegetable accompaniment.

Baked Samosas

Samosas are little pastry parcels stuffed with minced meat or a potato-based filling. They do take time to prepare and involve several stages, but they can be filled and shaped the night before and baked on the day.

PREPARATION TIME: 35 MINUTES
COOKING TIME: 50 MINUTES
MAKES 10–12

2 tbsp sunflower oil
1 onion, chopped
2 green chillies, finely chopped
¼ tsp salt
¼ tsp ground coriander
¼ tsp ground cumin
pinch of garam masala
200g sweet potatoes, peeled, boiled and roughly mashed
100g potatoes, peeled, boiled and roughly mashed
150g frozen mixed vegetables (such as peas and cauliflower), defrosted
handful of coriander leaves, washed and chopped

For the pastry
200g wholewheat flour
100g plain flour, plus extra for sealing and dusting
2 tbsp sunflower oil, plus extra for brushing
½ tsp carom (ajwain, ajowan) seeds

1 Heat the oil in a saucepan, then add the onion and fry for 5–7 minutes until translucent. Add the chillies and stir-fry for a minute or two. Add the salt, ground coriander, cumin and garam masala, and stir-fry for a minute.

2 Add the mashed potatoes, vegetables and coriander leaves and stir well to mix the ingredients together. Set aside.

3 To make the pastry, preheat the oven to 180°C/gas mark 4 and line a baking tray with baking parchment.

4 Place the flours, oil, carom seeds and 6–7 tablespoons of water into a large bowl. Knead for 5–8 minutes to make a firm, smooth dough.

5 Mix together a little plain flour and water to make a glue-like paste.

6 Heat a frying pan on a medium heat. Divide the dough into golf-ball-sized pieces and, on a floured surface, roll out into rounds about 3mm thick and 7.5cm in diameter.

7 Put a round of dough in the frying pan and cook for a minute on each side. This makes the pastry easier to handle. Remove from the pan with a spatula, place on a work surface or chopping board and cut each round in half.

8 Carefully lift one of the semi-circles and apply the flour-and-water paste to the straight edge.

9 Fold it to make a cone shape, sealing the pasted straight edge, then lift the cone with the tapered end at the bottom, and fill it with about 1 heaped teaspoon of the potato mixture.

10 Seal the samosa with a little more paste, pressing the edges firmly together to ensure there are no gaps, then folding over to seal. Repeat the process until all of the pastry has been used up.

11 Put the samosas on the lined baking tray and brush them on both sides with a little oil. Bake for 25–30 minutes, turning them once, until they are lightly browned. Serve hot with Gujarati Green Chutney (page 154).

Spiced Fruit Salad – Phalon ki Chaat

Chaat is the general term for the snacks sold at street stalls and shacks in India and Pakistan. Chaat dishes are often savoury and deep-fried and are normally eaten with chutneys and tangy and salty spices. This recipe uses seasonal fruits; it works as an appetiser rather than a dessert because of the zesty and sour spice combination.

PREPARATION TIME: 20 MINUTES
SERVES 4

1 tsp cumin seeds
1 orange, peeled and segmented
1 apple, cored and cubed
1 pear, cubed
2 bananas, sliced
½ pineapple, cubed
½ tsp rock salt
1 tbsp lemon juice
1 tbsp chopped mint leaves (optional)

1 Heat a frying pan on a medium heat and add the cumin seeds. When you can smell the aroma of the cumin, remove the pan from the heat and leave to cool.
2 Crush the cumin seeds to a coarse powder in a pestle and mortar.
3 Place all the fruits in a large bowl and mix them together.
4 Sprinkle with the rock salt, lemon juice and cumin seeds and garnish with mint, if using. Serve chilled.

Beetroot Crisps with Black Salt – Chukandar ki Wafers

Indian black rock salt is considered a cooling spice in Ayurveda, the ancient tradition of Indian medicine, and it adds a salty sour note to savoury dishes. The grains are more pinkish-grey than black in colour. If you cannot get hold of black salt, coarse sea salt works well.

PREPARATION TIME: 15 MINUTES
COOKING TIME: 15 MINUTES
SERVES 4

large bunch of beetroot (approx 450g)
olive oil for brushing
generous pinch of powdered black salt

1　Preheat the oven to 200°C/gas mark 6. Line a baking tray with greaseproof paper.
2　Cut off the stalks and leaves from the beetroots and discard. Wash and peel the beetroot and slice them thinly and as evenly as you can.
3　Place the beetroot slices on the baking tray in a single layer, not overlapping. (You will need to cook them in batches.) Brush lightly with olive oil and bake for about 10–15 minutes, checking from time to time to make sure they don't burn.
4　Remove from the oven and leave to cool until they become crisp. Sprinkle with the black salt and serve, or store in an airtight container for up to 6 days.

Turnip and Cumin Wedges – Masala Shalgam

Turnips belong to the cabbage family. Like other members of the cabbage family they are high in nutrients, low in calories and high in fibre, so they keep you feeling full. Early or young turnips are round and slightly squat, with a pearly white skin tinged with green and purple. They have a peppery flavour with a hint of sweetness.

PREPARATION TIME: 10 MINUTES
COOKING TIME: 35 MINUTES
SERVES 4

600g turnips, washed, trimmed and cut into wedges
½ tsp sea salt
½ tsp chilli flakes
½ tsp cumin seeds, crushed coarsely
generous pinch of coarsely ground black pepper
1 tsp lemon juice
2 tbsp olive oil

1 Preheat the oven to 180°C/gas mark 4.
2 Put the turnips in a saucepan, add water to cover and bring to the boil. Boil for 3–4 minutes, then drain.
3 In a bowl, mix the salt, chilli flakes, cumin seeds, black pepper, lemon juice and olive oil. Add the turnips and coat them with the mixture.
4 Spread the turnip wedges on a baking tray and bake for about 20–25 minutes until tender, turning them over once to ensure they are evenly browned.
5 Serve with Onion and Tomato Chutney (page 157).

Quick Lentil and Vegetable Soup – Dal Sabzi Shorba

Our bodies need a constant supply of protein for repair and growth of our organs and muscles. Split red lentils are one of the most inexpensive sources of protein, with a boost of dietary fibre. This spiced soup can be stored in the fridge for up to 3 days.

PREPARATION TIME: 10 MINUTES
COOKING TIME: 30 MINUTES
SERVES 4

200g split red lentils (masoor dal)
1 tbsp unsalted butter or olive oil
1 onion, chopped
200g cauliflower florets
1 green chilli, chopped
½ tsp ground cumin
½ tsp turmeric
pinch of asafoetida
¼ tsp salt (optional)
1 tsp peeled and grated fresh root ginger

1 Bring 500ml of water to the boil in a large saucepan on a high heat. Add the lentils and bring back to the boil. Partially cover the pan, reduce the heat to low and simmer, stirring occasionally, for 20–30 minutes until the mixture becomes mushy. Top up with boiling water if necessary.
2 Put the butter or oil in a frying pan on a medium heat. Add the onion and fry until soft.
3 Add the cauliflower and stir-fry for 2–3 minutes. Add the chilli and fry for a minute, then mix in the cumin, turmeric, asafoetida and salt, if using, and fry, stirring constantly, for 30 seconds.
4 Stir the spiced cauliflower mixture into the lentils, then cook for a further 2 minutes.
5 Add the ginger and stir through. Purée the mixture using a hand-held blender. Serve hot.

Chicken Mulligatawny Soup

The best-known Indian soup is the lentil-based mulligatawny, an anglicised version of an Indian broth that the Anglo-Indian community has been savouring for three centuries. This version uses chicken instead of lentils.

PREPARATION TIME: 10 MINUTES
COOKING TIME: 15 MINUTES
SERVES 4

2 tbsp olive oil
½ tsp cumin seeds
2 tbsp plain flour
500g skinless and boneless chicken, cooked and shredded
500ml Indian chicken stock (page 16)
¼ tsp salt (optional)
2 tbsp single cream
a few washed and chopped coriander leaves

1 Heat the oil in a large saucepan on a medium heat and add a few of the cumin seeds; when they crackle, add the remaining seeds and stir. Mix in the flour and stir for a minute until smooth.
2 Add the chicken, the stock and the salt, if using.
3 Simmer for 5–10 minutes until the mixture is quite thick.
4 Stir in the cream and serve immediately in warmed bowls, garnished with coriander leaves.

Curry Soup – Masala Shorba

Chilli peppers contain a compound called capsaicin which is able to act as a painkiller by depleting the brain of pain-signalling neurotransmitters. Red chilli flakes are also an appetite suppressant and they make a great substitute for salt. To make this thick spicy soup even more nutritious, add some cooked brown basmati rice.

PREPARATION TIME: 15 MINUTES
COOKING TIME: 30 MINUTES
SERVES 6

1 tbsp sunflower oil
1 onion, chopped
2 tbsp korma curry paste
pinch of dried chilli flakes
500g carrots, peeled and coarsely grated
100g split red lentils (masoor dal), rinsed
400ml light coconut milk
1 litre vegetable stock (use a low-salt stock cube if preferred)
¼ tsp freshly ground black pepper
a few washed and chopped coriander leaves

1　Heat the oil in a large saucepan on a medium heat. Add the onion and fry for 5–7 minutes until soft.
2　Add the curry paste and chilli flakes and fry for 2 minutes, then add the grated carrots, lentils, coconut milk and stock. Simmer for 15 minutes or until the lentils are soft (squash one against the side of the pan to check).
3　Purée the soup using a hand-held blender, adding the black pepper. Simmer for another 2–3 minutes, stirring occasionally.
4　Serve hot and scatter with the coriander leaves.

Tomato Consommé – Tamatar Rasedaar

Tomatoes contain some vitamin C and a pigment called lycopene, which is responsible for the deep red colour. It's an antioxidant that helps protect the body's cells from damage. *Tamatar* is the Hindi word for tomato and *ras* means juice or gravy. This recipe makes the most of seasonal crops of tomatoes and includes the spice coriander, which is believed to fight infections.

PREPARATION TIME: 15 MINUTES
COOKING TIME: 25 MINUTES
SERVES 4

750g ripe red tomatoes
2 tbsp olive oil
½ tsp cumin seeds
1 onion, finely chopped
2 garlic cloves, chopped
¼ tsp ground coriander
1 tsp peeled and grated fresh root ginger
1 tsp demerara sugar
¼ tsp salt (optional)
1 tsp unsalted butter
a few washed and chopped coriander leaves
¼ tsp freshly ground black pepper

1   Using a knife, score an 'X' on the tomatoes and immerse
    them in a bowl of just-boiled water for about a minute.
    Remove from the water, then peel off the skin and discard.
    Coarsely chop the tomatoes and set aside.

2   Heat the oil in a large saucepan on a medium heat and add a
    few of the cumin seeds; when they crackle, add the
    remaining seeds and stir. Add the onion and garlic and sauté
    for 4–5 minutes until soft.

3   Add the ground coriander, ginger, sugar and salt, if using, and
    mix well. Add the tomatoes and cook for 5–7 minutes until
    the tomatoes are soft and mushy and the mixture is quite
    thick.

4   Pour in 500ml of just-boiled water and cover. Simmer for
    7–10 minutes until the mixture has the consistency of double
    cream.

5   Leave to cool slightly, then, using a hand-held blender, blend
    until fairly smooth.

6   Gently reheat and mix in the butter. Serve in warmed bowls,
    garnished with coriander leaves and the black pepper, and
    accompanied by strips of chapati.

Indian-style Bubble and Squeak – Pav Bhaji

Toasted soft bread rolls topped with puréed spiced vegetables; I like to call this Indian-style bubble and squeak because you can use leftover vegetables and mashed potato to create a hot snack.

PREPARATION TIME: 20 MINUTES
COOKING TIME: 25 MINUTES
SERVES 4

500g frozen mixed vegetables (such as carrots, peas, cauliflower florets and green beans), defrosted
2 tbsp olive oil
1 onion, finely chopped
400g canned chopped tomatoes
1 tbsp tomato purée
½ tsp turmeric
½ tsp chilli powder
1½ tbsp pav bhaji masala spice blend (page 14)
200g potatoes, peeled, boiled and coarsely mashed
4 small soft granary or white rolls
1 tbsp butter, plus extra for spreading on the rolls

To serve
1 red onion, chopped
1 tbsp coriander leaves, washed and coarsely chopped
1 lemon, cut into wedges

1 Boil the mixed vegetables for 7–8 minutes until they are soft. Drain and set aside.
2 Heat the oil in a large saucepan on a medium heat. Add the onion and sauté for 5–7 minutes until lightly browned.
3 Add the tomatoes and simmer until the oil separates. Mix in the tomato purée, turmeric, chilli powder and pav bhaji spice blend and cook for 2–3 minutes.
4 Add the boiled vegetables and mashed potatoes and mash together using a potato masher, adding up to 125ml of water if the mixture seems too thick.
5 Slice each roll in half and spread a little butter on each side.
6 Heat a large frying pan and add the 1 tablespoon of butter. When the butter sizzles, add the rolls and toast on both sides until lightly browned. Remove and set aside.
7 Place the rolls on serving plates and top with the vegetable mixture. Sprinkle over the chopped onion and coriander, garnish with lemon wedges and serve hot.

Indian Cheese with Toasted Fennel Seeds – Paneer Saunfia Tikka

In India, fennel seeds (known as *saunf* in Hindi) are often chewed after a meal to aid digestion and also to sweeten the breath. They have a calming effect on the intestines and are thought to improve the absorption of nutrients from the foods we eat. The taste of fennel is sweet and similar to anise or liquorice.

PREPARATION TIME: 15 MINUTES
COOKING TIME: 12 MINUTES
SERVES 4

500g paneer, cut into 3cm cubes
2 red onions, cut into 3cm pieces
1 red pepper, cut into 3cm pieces
2 tbsp unsalted butter, melted
1 lemon, cut into wedges

For the marinade
80g coriander leaves, washed and coarsely chopped
2 green chillies, coarsely chopped
2 tsp fennel seeds, toasted and ground
1 tsp peeled and grated fresh root ginger
2 tbsp natural yogurt
1 tbsp gram flour (besan)
1 tsp lemon juice
½ tsp caster sugar
¼ tsp salt (optional)

1 To make the marinade, put all the ingredients in a blender or food processor and blend until smooth.
2 Place the marinade in a large bowl and add the paneer, onions and red pepper and mix well. Cover and put in the fridge for 15 minutes.
3 Meanwhile, soak 8–10 wooden skewers in water for 15 minutes. Preheat the grill until hot.
4 Thread the skewers with the paneer, onions and red pepper. Wrap the exposed ends of the skewers with foil to prevent them from burning.
5 Brush with melted butter and place under the hot grill for 10–12 minutes, turning occasionally until the paneer is golden brown.
6 Serve hot, with lemon wedges.

Vegetable Masala Sandwich

An important part of the spice trade since ancient times, black pepper was once known as black gold. Black pepper aids digestion and may help prevent obesity. This sandwich uses fresh ingredients combined with a minty relish: a typical packed lunch for many people in India.

PREPARATION TIME: 10 MINUTES
SERVES 4

8 tsp mint raita (page 152)
8 slices of wholewheat bread
18–20 cucumber slices
4 tomatoes, sliced
½ tsp freshly ground black pepper
pinch of powdered Himalayan or black salt (optional)

1 Spread the mint raita over each slice of bread.
2 Lay the cucumber slices on four slices of bread, and cover with the tomatoes. Sprinkle with the pepper and salt, if using.
3 Cover with the other four slices of bread, cut into triangles and serve.

Wholemeal Tarka Bread

Known as *rai* or *sarson* in Hindi, mustard seeds contain various antioxidants that may help slow down the ageing process. They are a popular flavouring for bean, vegetable and pickle dishes, and for snacks such as this seasoned bread.

PREPARATION TIME: 15 MINUTES
COOKING TIME: 10 MINUTES
SERVES 4

1 tbsp olive or sunflower oil
½ tsp brown or black mustard seeds
1 onion, chopped
1–2 green chillies, chopped
½ tsp turmeric
1 tbsp unsalted peanuts, crushed
¼ tsp ground cumin
¼ tsp salt (optional)
4 slices of wholemeal bread, cut into 2cm cubes
2 tbsp natural yogurt
1 tsp lemon juice
a few washed and chopped coriander leaves
1 tomato, finely chopped

1   Heat the oil in a small saucepan on a medium heat, then add a few of the mustard seeds; when they crackle, add the remaining seeds. Add the onion and chillies and stir for a minute. Then add the turmeric, peanuts, cumin and salt, if using, and continue to stir-fry for 1 minute.
2   Add the bread cubes and sauté for 2 minutes until lightly golden on the edges.
3   Add the yogurt and lemon juice, stirring continuously, and cook for 2 more minutes. Serve immediately, sprinkled with coriander leaves and chopped tomato.

Vegetable Chop

'Vegetable chop' is a popular vegetarian delight from the street stalls of Kolkata. These croquettes are often deep-fried but I've created a 'sauté' version which is less greasy and, if I may say so, much tastier.

PREPARATION TIME: 20 MINUTES
COOKING TIME: 30 MINUTES
MAKES 8 CROQUETTES

2 beetroots, washed and peeled and chopped into 2cm pieces
2 carrots, peeled and chopped into 2cm pieces
2 potatoes, peeled and chopped into 2cm pieces
2 tbsp sunflower oil
30g peanuts, coarsely crushed
2 tsp peeled and grated fresh root ginger
2 tsp curry powder spice blend (page 10)
¼ tsp chilli powder
¼ tsp salt (optional)
½ tsp caster sugar (optional)

1 Put the beetroots, carrots and potatoes in a saucepan and add enough water to cover them. Bring to the boil and cook for 15–20 minutes until they are soft enough to mash.
2 Drain them and place in a bowl. Using a masher or a fork, coarsely mash the vegetables and set aside.
3 Add 1 teaspoon of the oil to the saucepan, then add the peanuts and ginger and sauté for a couple of minutes.
4 Add the mashed vegetables, the curry powder, chilli powder, salt and sugar, if using. Mix well until the mixture becomes thick and leaves the sides of the pan. Leave to cool.
5 Using wet hands, take golf-ball-sized pieces of the mixture and shape into oval croquettes about 2cm thick.
6 Heat the remaining oil in a frying pan and fry the croquettes for 2–3 minutes on each side until they turn a little darker.
7 Drain on kitchen paper. Serve with Tomato Chutney (page 160).

Lentil Kebabs – Chana Dal Kebabs

Chana dal or Bengal gram is a variety of chickpea that is sold hulled and split; it is one of the most important pulses in Indian cooking and is very nutritious: high in protein and dietary fibre and a good source of iron. It has many culinary uses; for example it is ground to produce the flour known as besan, which is used for both sweet and savoury dishes. These kebabs are a delicious vegetarian option for the barbecue.

PREPARATION TIME: 15 MINUTES, PLUS 1 HOUR SOAKING
COOKING TIME: 30 MINUTES
MAKES 8-10 KEBABS

100g yellow split peas (chana dal or Bengal gram)
2 green chillies, chopped
2 garlic cloves
2 tsp tomato purée
a few coriander leaves, washed and chopped
1 tbsp rapeseed oil
1 tsp lemon juice
1 tbsp rice flour
¼ tsp ground cinnamon
¼ tsp salt
1 small onion, finely chopped, or 2 spring onions, finely chopped

1 Soak the chana dal in cold water for 1 hour.
2 Drain the chana dal and place in a saucepan, add 400ml of boiling water and boil for 10–15 minutes until soft.
3 Meanwhile, soak 8–10 wooden skewers in water for 15 minutes.
4 Drain the chana dal and place in a food processor along with all the remaining ingredients – except the onion – and blend to a coarse paste.
5 Add the onion or spring onions and mix well. Using wet hands, take a golf-ball-sized piece of the mixture and press it tightly around a skewer in a sausage shape. Repeat with the remaining mixture.
6 Place under a preheated grill or on a barbecue, and cook for 10–15 minutes on each side or until the kebabs become a little darker. Serve with Tomato Chutney (page 160).

Lentil Pancakes – Moong Dal Chila

Ginger has been valued as a herbal remedy for centuries, in particular for warming chills, aiding digestion and preventing nausea. When preparing bean and lentil dishes, ginger may help to counteract the feeling of bloatedness that occurs when consuming pulses.

PREPARATION TIME: 15 MINUTES, PLUS 3 HOURS SOAKING
COOKING TIME: 15 MINUTES
MAKES APPROXIMATELY 10 PANCAKES

250g yellow split mung beans (moong dal)
2 tsp peeled and grated fresh root ginger
1–2 small green chillies, finely chopped
¼ tsp asafoetida
¼ tsp turmeric
1 onion, finely chopped
2 tbsp coriander leaves, finely chopped
¼ tsp salt (optional)
3 tbsp olive oil

1 Wash the dal and place in a bowl. Add cold water to cover the dal and soak for 2–3 hours.
2 Drain the dal and reserve the water. Add the ginger, chillies, asafoetida and turmeric to the dal and place in a blender with about 125ml of the reserved water. Blend to make a smooth batter.
3 Pour the batter into a bowl and add the onion, coriander leaves and salt, if using, and mix well.
4 Heat 1 teaspoon of the oil in a frying pan. Drop a tablespoon of batter in the centre of the pan. Using the back of a ladle, spread the batter into a circle approximately 10cm in diameter. Cook for 2–3 minutes on each side until brown spots appear on the surface.
5 Taste the pancake to check the seasoning, adjust if necessary and then use the remaining batter to make more pancakes in the same way. Serve hot with Gujarati Green Chutney (page 154).

Kidney Bean Kebabs – Rajma Galouti Kebab

Like other pulses, kidney beans are an excellent source of fibre, which, among other health benefits, prevents blood sugar levels from rising too quickly after a meal. These kebabs show the influence of Mughal cuisine, in which luxurious ingredients such as saffron and rose were commonly used.

PREPARATION TIME: 10 MINUTES
COOKING TIME: 15 MINUTES
MAKES 8 SMALL KEBABS

10–15 unsalted cashew nuts
2 tbsp rose water
5–6 saffron strands
1 tbsp olive or sunflower oil
1 tsp peeled and grated fresh root ginger
2 garlic cloves, crushed
1 green chilli, finely chopped
400g can kidney beans, rinsed and drained
¼ tsp ground white pepper
pinch of salt (optional)
pinch of garam masala
1 tsp lemon juice

1 Heat a small pan on a medium heat and add the cashew nuts. Sauté for a few minutes until they turn slightly darker in colour. Leave them to cool. Once cooled, crush them in a pestle and mortar until they are finely ground.

2 Place the rose water in a bowl and add the saffron. Set aside.

3 Heat a saucepan on a medium heat, add the oil, then add the ginger and garlic and sauté for a few seconds. Mix in the chilli and sauté for 1 minute. Add the kidney beans and cook for 3–4 minutes, mashing the mixture as you cook.

4 Add the ground cashew nuts and stir-fry for 4–5 minutes. Add the white pepper and salt, if using, and stir-fry for another 4–5 minutes. Mix in the garam masala and lemon juice.

5 Take the mixture off the heat and leave until it's cool enough to handle. Shape into eight golf-ball-sized patties. Serve with Onion and Tomato Chutney (page 157).

Egg Curry

This curry is a favourite street snack in India, especially in Mumbai. Eggs are an excellent source of protein, along with vitamin D to help keep bones and teeth strong, plenty of B vitamins and other nutrients. To check whether an egg is fresh, place it in water: if it sinks it's fresh, if it's stale it will float.

PREPARATION TIME: 10 MINUTES
COOKING TIME: 30 MINUTES
SERVES 4

6 eggs
2 tbsp olive oil
2 onions, finely chopped
3–4 garlic cloves, crushed
1 green chilli, finely chopped
1 tsp peeled and grated fresh root ginger
¼ tsp turmeric
1 tsp ground coriander
1 tsp ground cumin
1 tsp medium hot curry powder, or use the curry powder spice blend (page 10)
¼ tsp salt (optional)
3 tomatoes, finely chopped, or 400g canned chopped tomatoes, blended
a few washed and chopped coriander leaves

1. Put the eggs into a saucepan of cold water, bring to a simmer and simmer for 8–10 minutes. Cool them under cold running water, then peel and set aside.
2. Heat a large saucepan on a medium heat and add the oil. Add the onions and garlic and fry for 7–9 minutes until lightly browned.
3. Add the chilli and cook for a further 3 minutes.
4. Add the ginger, turmeric, ground coriander, cumin, curry powder and salt, if using. Leave to cook for 2 minutes, then add the tomatoes and cook for 2 minutes more.
5. Add 200ml water and stir in. Carefully add the eggs and simmer for 3 minutes.
6. Garnish with the coriander leaves and serve hot with chapatis.

Chicken Reshmi Kebabs

Skinless chicken breast is a good source of protein and is low in fat, which makes it ideal for maintaining a healthy weight. Dried fenugreek leaves are easily available in Asian grocery stores and online spice shops. They add a gentle bitter note to these delicately flavoured kebabs.

PREPARATION TIME: 10 MINUTES, PLUS 2 HOURS MARINATING
COOKING TIME: 20 MINUTES
MAKES 10-12 KEBABS

2 tsp fennel seeds
4 skinless and boneless chicken breasts, cut into 2cm pieces
1 tsp garam masala
2 green chillies, finely chopped
2 garlic cloves, crushed
1 tsp peeled and grated fresh root ginger
4 tbsp single cream
3 tbsp natural yogurt
1 tbsp dried fenugreek leaves (kasoori methi)
2 tbsp gram flour (besan)
2 tsp lemon juice
¼ tsp salt (optional)
pinch of saffron (optional)
sunflower oil for brushing

1　Heat a small pan on a medium heat and add the fennel seeds. Toast for a minute, shaking the pan from time to time to prevent them from burning. Tip them on to a plate and leave to cool. Place in a pestle and mortar and grind to a fine powder.

2　In a bowl large enough to hold the chicken, mix the ground fennel seeds with the garam masala, chillies, garlic, ginger, cream, yogurt, fenugreek leaves, gram flour, lemon juice, salt and saffron, if using. Whisk with a fork to remove any lumps.

3　Prick the chicken pieces so that the marinade can seep right through the chicken. Add the chicken to the marinade and mix well. Cover the bowl and marinate for at least 2 hours or preferably overnight.

4　Soak 10–12 wooden skewers in cold water for 30 minutes.

5　Thread the chicken on to the skewers. Wrap the exposed ends of the skewers with foil to prevent them from burning.

6　Brush with a little oil and grill or barbecue for 12–15 minutes, turning them once until the chicken is cooked right through. Serve hot with Mint Raita (page 152).

Fish Kebabs – Mahi Ajwaini Tikka

Ajwain or ajowan (also known as carom) is a tiny oval ridged fruit (often referred to as a seed) with a pungent fragrance reminiscent of thyme. It comes from a herb belonging to the cumin and parsley family and has a hot and sharp taste on the tongue. It has been used for its culinary and medicinal properties for centuries, particularly in traditional Indian Ayurvedic medicine. It's considered to be an instant remedy for indigestion and stomach ache. The combination of fish with ajwain is popular in northern Indian cuisine.

PREPARATION TIME: 25 MINUTES
COOKING TIME: 10 MINUTES
MAKES 8-10 KEBABS

8 white fish fillets, such as coley, cod or pollack
1 tbsp lemon juice
4–6 garlic cloves, crushed
1 tbsp peeled and grated fresh root ginger
2 tsp ajwain (ajowan, carom seeds), toasted and ground
½ tsp ground white pepper
2 tbsp olive oil

1 Cut the fish into 4cm pieces.
2 Mix the lemon juice, garlic, ginger, ajwain, pepper and oil in a bowl large enough to hold the fish. Put the fish in the bowl and coat evenly with the marinade. Cover the bowl and place in the fridge for 15 minutes.
3 Meanwhile, soak 8–10 wooden skewers in water for 15 minutes.
4 Preheat the grill until hot. Thread the fish on to the skewers and grill for 10 minutes, turning occasionally, until cooked. Serve hot with a crisp green salad.

Chargrilled Lamb Chops – Burra Kebab

Burra literally means big; this delicacy is a large lamb chop marinated in spices and then cooked over hot charcoal. Many street places in Delhi specialise in this, and it also appears on the menu of Delhi's world-famous Bukhara restaurant.

PREPARATION TIME: 5 MINUTES, PLUS AT LEAST 2 HOURS MARINATING
COOKING TIME: 5 MINUTES
SERVES 4

4 garlic cloves, crushed
1 tbsp grated fresh root ginger
1 tbsp lemon juice
1 tbsp sunflower or olive oil
½ tsp chilli powder
1 tsp ground cumin
¼ tsp salt (optional)
8 lamb chops

1 Put the garlic in a bowl with the ginger, lemon juice, oil, spices and seasoning. Using a hand-held blender, blitz to a smooth paste, then use to coat the lamb chops on both sides. Leave in the fridge to marinate for a couple of hours or overnight.
2 Heat a barbecue until hot. Barbecue the chops for 3–4 minutes on each side until cooked. Alternatively, preheat a grill until hot and cook the chops until lightly browned. Serve hot.

Smoked Paprika Lamb Kebabs

Paprika is the spice produced from drying certain varieties of red peppers. The heat intensity is very mild and works well in kebab dishes and as a natural food colouring.

PREPARATION TIME: 15 MINUTES
COOKING TIME: 30 MINUTES
SERVES 4

500g lean minced lamb
2 spring onions, chopped
2 sprigs of rosemary, leaves washed and chopped
1 tsp smoked paprika
4 garlic cloves, crushed
2 tbsp olive oil
½ tsp plain flour

For the yogurt dressing
4 tbsp natural yogurt, whisked
4–5 mint leaves, washed and chopped
1 garlic clove, crushed

To serve
2 wholemeal pitta breads, cut in half
1 red pepper, chopped
1 yellow pepper, chopped

1   Place the lamb in a bowl and add the spring onions, rosemary, smoked paprika, garlic and 1 tablespoon of the oil. Mix well, then add the flour and mix together.

2   Using wet hands, divide the mince into eight equal parts. Shape each into a flat round patty about 1.5cm thick.

3   Heat a frying pan on a medium heat and add the remaining 1 tablespoon of oil.

4   Place two, three or four patties at a time in the pan (depending on the size of your pan) and fry for 5 minutes on one side until golden brown, then turn over and fry the other side for 5 minutes or until cooked through. Drain on kitchen paper.

5   To make the dressing, mix the yogurt, mint and garlic together in a bowl.

6   Place two lamb patties in each pitta pocket. Put some of the red and yellow pepper into each pocket and top with a tablespoon of the yogurt dressing.

Minced Lamb Kebabs – Seekh Kebabs

The seekh kebab is one of the best-known tandoori dishes in Indian cooking. There are many recipes for these kebabs and each cook adds his or her own ingredients to give it a special and possibly unique flavour. Below is a basic recipe which uses a paste made of fried onions for a touch of northern Indian sweetness that reflects my father's roots.

PREPARATION TIME: 15 MINUTES
COOKING TIME: 25 MINUTES
MAKES 10-12 KEBABS

500g lean minced lamb
2 tbsp peeled and grated fresh root ginger
2 green chillies, finely chopped
1 tsp garam masala
1 tsp paprika
¼ tsp salt
2 tbsp sunflower or olive oil, plus extra for brushing the grill rack
1 onion, finely chopped

1   Put the mince in a large bowl and add the ginger, chillies, garam masala, paprika and salt and mix well.
2   Heat the oil in a large frying pan on a medium heat. Add the onion and fry, stirring occasionally, for 5–7 minutes until soft. Leave to cool.
3   Soak 12 wooden skewers in cold water for 15 minutes.
4   Preheat the grill until hot. Lightly grease the grill rack.
5   Add the cooled onion to the lamb mixture and mix thoroughly. Divide the mixture into 10–12 equal portions. Using wet hands, shape each portion around a skewer in a sausage shape, smoothing over the 'seam'.
6   Place the skewers under the grill and grill for 10–15 minutes, turning occasionally, until the meat is cooked through. Serve hot with Onion and Tomato Chutney (page 157).

....

CHAPTER 3

Vegetables

Vegetarian food is seen as a naturally healthy way of eating. However, in recent decades, with the advent of fast foods and the adoption of Western dietary lifestyles, there has been an increase in the number of vegetable dishes made by deep frying. Not only does this add to the calorie density of the foods, which is not good news if you are watching your weight, but when oil is heated to the high temperatures needed for deep frying, the chemical structure of the oil is damaged, making it very bad for your health. Some of the dishes in this chapter are baked, others are sautéed in a little oil for a short amount of time to retain the vibrant appearance, taste and texture of the vegetables. Frozen vegetables can be just as healthy as fresh ones, since they retain many of the original nutrients.

Spiced Sautéed Potatoes – Aloo Tuk

The key to weight management is to eat foods that keep you feeling full for longer, such as the complex carbohydrates found in potatoes, which provide the body with a valuable source of fuel. This dish is typical of Sindhi cuisine, from the province of Sindh in Pakistan. A Sindhi meal generally consists of a bread and two other dishes, one with a sauce and one dry, such as these spiced potatoes.

PREPARATION TIME: 10 MINUTES
COOKING TIME: 40 MINUTES
SERVES 4

500g baby or new potatoes, such as Charlotte
2 tbsp sunflower or olive oil
¼ tsp salt (optional)
¼–½ tsp paprika or Kashmiri chilli powder
3 tsp lemon juice
a few washed and chopped coriander leaves

1   Wash the potatoes but do not peel them. Put them in a saucepan, cover with boiling water and boil for 15–20 minutes until just tender. Drain and set aside.
2   Preheat the oven to 180°C/gas mark 4.
3   When the potatoes have cooled down slightly, gently squash each one with a potato masher or the back of a large spoon, being careful not to break them up. Place them on a baking tray.
4   In a small bowl, mix the oil with the salt, if using, the paprika or Kashmiri chilli powder and 2 teaspoons of the lemon juice. Brush the tops of the potatoes with the dressing and place in the oven.
5   Bake for 20 minutes until they're lightly browned. Sprinkle with the remaining 1 teaspoon of lemon juice and garnish with the coriander leaves.

Baked Aubergines

Aubergines are rich in dietary fibre and, like many purple-coloured vegetables and fruits, contain a phytochemical known as nasunin that may help to lower cholesterol. When buying aubergines they should be smooth, shiny, firm and heavy.

PREPARATION TIME: 20 MINUTES
COOKING TIME: 45 MINUTES
SERVES 4

500g baby aubergines, washed
2 tsp ground cumin
½ tsp garam masala
¼ tsp chilli powder
¼ tsp salt (optional)
2 tsp peeled and grated fresh root ginger
4–5 garlic cloves, crushed
2 tbsp malt vinegar
1 tbsp olive or rapeseed oil

1   Preheat the oven to 180°C/gas mark 4. Line a baking tray with foil.
2   Cut lengthways through each aubergine to create a long slit, while keeping the aubergines intact; set aside.
3   In a bowl large enough to hold the aubergines, combine the cumin, garam masala, chilli powder, salt, if using, ginger, garlic and vinegar. Mix well.
4   Add the aubergines and stir them around in the spice mixture, ensuring the insides of the aubergines are coated with the spices. Leave to marinate for 10 minutes.
5   Place them on the lined baking tray, sprinkle over the oil and bake for 40–45 minutes until the aubergines are soft. Serve hot with chapatis and Pomegranate Yogurt Salad (page 180).

Beetroot Curry – Chukandar ka Saalan

Beetroots may help to lower blood pressure because they contain a compound that relaxes and dilates blood vessels, thus improving blood flow. In Indian cooking, beetroot is considered a superfood and is used to make drinks, chutneys and curries.

PREPARATION TIME: 15 MINUTES
COOKING TIME: 35 MINUTES
SERVES 4

350g small beetroots, washed, peeled and trimmed
2 tbsp unsalted butter
2cm piece of cinnamon stick
5–6 curry leaves
1 onion, finely chopped
2 green chillies, finely chopped
2 garlic cloves, sliced
1 tsp ground coriander
1 tsp chilli powder
1 tbsp white vinegar
1 tsp caster sugar
200ml light coconut milk

1 Cut the beetroots into 1cm pieces; set aside.
2 Heat the butter in a heavy-based saucepan on a medium heat. Add the cinnamon and curry leaves. When the mixture begins to sizzle, mix in the onion and fry for 6–8 minutes or until translucent.
3 Add the chillies and garlic, stir and cook for 3 minutes or until fragrant.
4 Add the beetroot and the remaining ingredients. Cover and simmer on a very low heat, stirring occasionally, for 15–20 minutes or until the beetroots are tender. Serve hot with plain basmati rice.

Stuffed Peppers – Bharwan Mirch

Stuffed peppers look appetising, they are packed with vitamin C and they are low in calories. This recipe uses leftover mashed potatoes which are spiced and then packed into the peppers.

PREPARATION TIME: 20 MINUTES
COOKING TIME: 30 MINUTES
SERVES 4

4 red, yellow or green peppers
3 tbsp sunflower oil
1 onion, finely chopped
½ tsp turmeric
1 tsp ground coriander
½ tsp mango powder (amchur)
½ tsp chilli powder
¼ tsp salt (optional)
500g potatoes, boiled and roughly mashed

1 Slice the tops off the peppers and remove the seeds. Keep the tops and set them aside.
2 Preheat the oven to 180°C/gas mark 4. Line a baking tray with foil.
3 Heat the oil in a frying pan on a medium heat, add the onion and fry for 5–6 minutes until lightly browned.
4 Add the turmeric, coriander, mango powder, chilli powder and salt, if using, and mix well. Then add the potatoes and cook for 2 minutes. Remove from the heat.
5 Using a spoon, fill the peppers generously with the potato mixture and cover with the pepper tops.
6 Carefully place the peppers on the lined baking tray and bake for 20–25 minutes until the peppers are lightly browned. Serve hot with Mint Raita (page 152).

Broccoli with Cumin and Garlic – Broccoli Bhaji

Broccoli is an excellent source of vitamin C and also vitamin K, which is often overlooked in the repertoire of vitamins: it plays an important role in blood clotting and the building of bones. A diet lacking in green leafy vegetables can lead to osteoporosis and hardening of the arteries. This recipe is a quick stir-fry using Indian spices, including asafoetida to aid digestion.

PREPARATION TIME: 10 MINUTES
COOKING TIME: 10 MINUTES
SERVES 4

2 tbsp olive oil
½ tsp black mustard seeds
½ tsp cumin seeds
pinch of asafoetida
2 garlic cloves, crushed
½ tsp turmeric
300g broccoli, cut into florets
¼ tsp salt (optional)

1   Heat the oil in a heavy-based pan on a medium heat and add a few of the mustard and cumin seeds; when they crackle, add the remaining seeds and the asafoetida and stir. Add the garlic and turmeric and stir for a minute.
2   Mix in the broccoli and sauté for 4–5 minutes until the broccoli softens slightly.
3   Add the salt, if using, and mix, then add a couple of tablespoons of water and reduce the heat. Cook for another 3 minutes. Serve hot with a lentil dish.

Courgettes with Cumin – Zucchini ki Sabzi

Courgettes are summer squash, a good source of dietary fibre. When picking courgettes, make sure they are firm, with shiny skins. Squashes are big in Indian vegetarian cuisine and in this recipe the warmth of the cumin mingles with the soft buttery taste of the courgettes.

PREPARATION TIME: 15 MINUTES
COOKING TIME: 20 MINUTES
SERVES 4

3 tbsp sunflower or olive oil
1 tsp cumin seeds
1 onion, chopped
3–4 garlic cloves, chopped
1 green chilli, finely chopped
1 tomato, chopped
½ tsp turmeric
1 tsp ground coriander
¼ tsp salt (optional)
600g courgettes, washed and cut into 1cm thick slices
2 tsp peeled and grated fresh root ginger
¼ tsp garam masala
a few washed and chopped coriander leaves

1 Heat a saucepan on a medium heat and add the oil. Add a few cumin seeds; when they crackle, add the remaining seeds and stir, then add the onion and fry for a minute.
2 Add the garlic and chilli and fry for 5–7 minutes until the mixture turns golden brown.
3 Mix in the tomato and cook for 2–3 minutes until it becomes thick.
4 Stir in the turmeric, coriander and salt, if using. Add the courgettes and ginger and fry for 5–6 minutes.
5 Sprinkle with the garam masala. Garnish with coriander leaves and serve hot with chapatis and a lentil curry.

Sweet Potato Dhansak

Dhansak is a Parsi dish from western India, based on pulses and vegetables: 'dhan' refers to the pulses and 'sak' means vegetables; in this recipe they are puréed together in a spicy sauce. Sweet potatoes are high in beta-carotene, which the body converts into vitamin A, which is essential for protecting our eyes, skin and immune system. They also contain vitamin C, which plays an important role in maintaining healthy bones, teeth and skin. Their natural sugars are slowly released into the bloodstream without the blood sugar spikes that are linked to weight gain.

PREPARATION TIME: 15 MINUTES
COOKING TIME: 1 HOUR
SERVES 4

100g yellow split peas (chana dal)
100g yellow split mung beans (moong dal)
200g sweet potatoes, peeled and quartered
200g carrots, chopped
1 tsp lemon juice
3 tbsp butter, ghee or olive oil
2 tsp peeled and grated fresh root ginger
4 garlic cloves, chopped
2 green chillies, slit lengthways
2 onions, chopped
1 tsp ground cumin
1 tsp ground coriander
¼ tsp ground cinnamon
½ tsp turmeric
¼ tsp salt (optional)
2 tomatoes, finely chopped

1 Bring 750ml of water to the boil in a saucepan. Add the split peas and mung beans and bring the water back to the boil. Partially cover the pan, reduce the heat and simmer, stirring occasionally, for 35–40 minutes until the mixture is mushy. Top up with boiling water if necessary.

2 Meanwhile, bring another large saucepan of water to the boil. Add the sweet potatoes and carrots and boil for 15–20 minutes until they are both very tender and the potatoes almost falling apart. Drain well.

3 Pour the split peas and beans and any remaining water into a blender. Add the drained sweet potatoes and carrots, add the lemon juice and blend to a thick purée. Set aside.

4 Heat the butter or oil in a large saucepan on a medium to low heat. Add the ginger, garlic, chillies and onions and fry, stirring occasionally, for 7–9 minutes until the onions are lightly browned.

5 Stir in the cumin, coriander, cinnamon, turmeric and salt, if using. Then add the tomatoes and cook for 1 minute, stirring occasionally.

6 Stir in the lentil and vegetable mixture and cook for a further 2 minutes. Serve hot with plain basmati rice or chapatis.

Celeriac Dhansak

Celeriac is a creamy coloured, knobbly, nutty-tasting root vegetable that is often overlooked. It's closely related to leafy celery and is rich in vitamin K – necessary for healthy bones. To prepare it, you need to trim off any green leafy bits and straggly roots, then peel or slice off and discard the tough exterior (about a quarter of the vegetable will be tossed out).

To make a celeriac dhansak, use 200g peeled and quartered celeriac instead of the sweet potatoes.

Sautéed Marrow – Ghia ki Sabzi

Marrow is a type of squash, related to courgettes and pumpkins, and this dish is a robust creation from the kitchens of Punjab in northern India. Turmeric brings a rich yellow colour and a number of powerful antioxidant compounds that support the immune system.

PREPARATION TIME: 20 MINUTES
COOKING TIME: 30 MINUTES
SERVES 4

1kg marrow, washed
3 tbsp olive oil
1 onion, finely chopped
2 green chillies, finely chopped
4 garlic cloves, chopped
1 tsp turmeric
1 tsp ground coriander
½ tsp ground cumin
¼ tsp freshly ground black pepper
¼ tsp salt (optional)
200g tomatoes, finely chopped
1 tsp peeled and grated fresh root ginger

1   Top and tail the marrow. Cut it in half, then cut it lengthways and scoop out the seeds. Chop into 3cm pieces.
2   Heat the oil in a large saucepan on a medium heat. Add the onion and sauté for 7–9 minutes until lightly browned. Add the chillies and garlic and gently fry for 5 minutes until golden.
3   Add the turmeric, coriander, cumin, pepper and salt, if using, and stir for a minute. Mix in the tomatoes and cook for a couple of minutes.
4   Add the marrow pieces and mix well. Cover and cook gently for 15 minutes until the marrow is tender.
5   Stir in the ginger. Serve hot with Carom Flatbreads (page 172).

Butternut Squash with Green Chilli

Squashes and pumpkins originally came from the Americas and they are found in a huge variety of colours and sizes. Butternut squash is a winter squash with orange-coloured flesh and a sweetish, slightly honey-like flavour. It is rich in potassium, which can help decrease blood pressure by balancing the effects of sodium.

PREPARATION TIME: 10 MINUTES
COOKING TIME: 20 MINUTES
SERVES 4

1 butternut squash (approximately 800g), peeled and cut
   into 4cm cubes
3 tbsp olive or rapeseed oil
½ tsp brown mustard seeds
pinch of asafoetida
¼ tsp salt (optional)
3 green chillies, finely chopped
2 tsp peeled and grated fresh root ginger
1 tsp ground cumin
½ tsp turmeric
2 tsp lemon juice

1 Preheat the oven to 180°C/gas mark 4.
2 Place the squash pieces in a roasting tin and sprinkle over
   about 1 tablespoon of the oil. Roast for about 15 minutes
   until almost tender. Remove from the oven and set aside.
3 Heat a large saucepan on a medium heat and add the
   remaining 2 tablespoons of oil. Tip in a few of the mustard
   seeds; when they crackle, add the remaining seeds. Add the
   asafoetida, the salt, if using, green chillies, ginger, cumin and
   turmeric. Add the squash and sauté in the spice mixture for
   2 minutes until well combined.
4 Sprinkle over the lemon juice. Serve hot with chapatis.

Green Beans Foogath

Foogath is the name for the dry vegetable side dishes served in southern India. Vegetables such as beans, cabbage, cauliflower or greens are parboiled then flavoured with spices such as mustard seeds, curry leaves, dried red or fresh green chillies, and grated coconut. Green beans are a good source of many vitamins and minerals, and they also contain flavonoids that can help reduce the risk of heart disease.

PREPARATION TIME: 15 MINUTES
COOKING TIME: 15 MINUTES
SERVES 4

350g green beans, topped and tailed and cut into 3cm pieces
2 tbsp sunflower oil
5–6 curry leaves (optional)
½ tsp brown mustard seeds
1–2 onions, finely chopped
3–4 garlic cloves, chopped
2 tsp peeled and grated fresh root ginger
2 green chillies, slit lengthways
1 tbsp unsweetened desiccated coconut
1 tsp lime juice

1 Boil the beans for about 5 minutes (they should still be quite crisp). Drain and set aside.
2 Heat the oil in a frying pan on a medium heat and add the curry leaves, if using, followed by a few of the mustard seeds. When they crackle, add the remaining seeds, then tip in the onions and fry for 4–5 minutes.
3 Stir in the garlic and sauté for 2 minutes.
4 Add the ginger and chillies and mix. Stir in the coconut and cook for a further minute.
5 Sprinkle with the lime juice and serve hot.

Green Beans with Garlic and Lemon

Mustard seeds are to southern, south-western and eastern India what cumin seeds are to the north. Used to season just about every savoury preparation, their hot and nutty flavour is brought out once they are heated in oil. This simple dish is a great way to make the most of seasonal green beans. If you prefer the beans to be softer, parboil them for 5–7 minutes and drain before adding them to the onion mixture.

PREPARATION TIME: 15 MINUTES
COOKING TIME: 10 MINUTES
SERVES 4

3 tbsp sunflower or olive oil
½ tsp brown or black mustard seeds
3 garlic cloves, chopped
2 green chillies, finely chopped
1 onion, finely chopped
400g green beans, topped and tailed
1 tsp ground cumin
¼ tsp salt (optional)
juice of ½ a lemon
¼ tsp freshly ground black pepper

1   Heat the oil in a large frying pan on a medium heat. Add the mustard seeds and fry, stirring constantly, for 30 seconds or until they splutter. Add the garlic, chillies and onion and fry, stirring frequently, for 3 minutes until the onion is soft.
2   Add the beans and fry for 1 minute.
3   Stir in the cumin and salt, if using, and continue frying for 2–3 minutes or until the beans are just tender.
4   Sprinkle with the lemon juice and black pepper just before serving.

Green Peppers with Tomatoes – Shimla Mirch Masala

This is a lightly sautéed combination of peppers with cumin and coriander that makes a good accompaniment to meat dishes. Green peppers are packed with vitamin C and E, which help protect cells from damage. Cumin is widely believed to relieve cold symptoms such as a sore throat and congestion and also to reduce nausea.

PREPARATION TIME: 15 MINUTES
COOKING TIME: 12 MINUTES
SERVES 4

2 tbsp olive oil
½ tsp cumin seeds
1 onion, sliced
2 tomatoes, chopped
½ tsp ground coriander
¼ tsp turmeric
¼ tsp salt (optional)
3 green peppers, sliced
pinch of garam masala
a few washed and chopped coriander leaves

1 Heat the oil in a large frying pan on a medium heat and add a few of the cumin seeds; when they start to crackle, add the remaining seeds. Add the onion and sauté for 3–4 minutes until translucent.
2 Add the tomatoes, ground coriander, turmeric and salt, if using, and mix. Cook for 3–4 minutes until the mixture is quite dry and thick.
3 Toss in the peppers and fry for a couple of minutes.
4 Add the garam masala and sprinkle with the coriander leaves. Serve hot with chapatis.

Mixed Vegetable Curry – Thoran

Thoran is a dry vegetable dish from southern India. All kinds of vegetables can be used, such as cabbage and other leafy greens; the spices transform the vegetables into a delicious dish that can be served as the main attraction.

PREPARATION TIME: 15 MINUTES
COOKING TIME: 20 MINUTES
SERVES 4

2 tbsp coconut oil
½ tsp brown or black mustard seeds
pinch of asafoetida
8–10 curry leaves (optional)
1 onion, finely chopped
2 green chillies, finely chopped
¼ tsp turmeric
¼ tsp salt (optional)
pinch of freshly ground black pepper
150g carrots, cut into batons
100g frozen peas, defrosted
100g fine green beans, topped, tailed and cut into 3cm pieces
1 tsp peeled and grated fresh root ginger

1   Heat the oil in a large pan on a medium heat and add a few of the mustard seeds; when they crackle, add the remaining seeds and stir, then add the asafoetida and curry leaves, if using.
2   Add the onion and sauté for 5–7 minutes until lightly browned.
3   Add the chillies and stir, then mix in the turmeric, salt, if using, and the black pepper.
4   Add the carrots, peas and beans and mix. Add 60ml of water, cover and cook on a low heat for 6–8 minutes until the vegetables are tender.
5   Sprinkle over the ginger and serve hot with rice and a lentil dish.

Spinach with Indian Cheese – Palak Paneer

Paneer is a full-fat fresh cheese used in Indian cooking. It is made with lemon juice or vinegar (rather than animal-derived rennet) and so is suitable for vegetarians, and it is a good source of protein and calcium. *Palak* is the Hindi word for spinach; you may also see this dish described as *saag paneer*, *saag* being a more general term for green leafy vegetables.

PREPARATION TIME: 10 MINUTES
COOKING TIME: 20 MINUTES
SERVES 4

2 tbsp olive oil
1 onion, chopped
2 garlic cloves, chopped
2 green chillies, chopped
½ tsp turmeric
½ tsp ground cumin
¼ tsp ground coriander
1 tsp peeled and grated fresh root ginger
1 tsp tomato purée
¼ tsp salt (optional)
250g washed and chopped fresh or defrosted frozen spinach
1 tsp unsalted butter
100g paneer, cut into 3cm cubes
a few washed and chopped coriander leaves

1 Heat the oil in a saucepan on a medium heat. Add the onion and fry for 5–7 minutes until lightly golden.
2 Add the garlic and chillies and cook for a couple of minutes.
3 Stir in the turmeric, cumin, ground coriander, ginger, tomato purée and salt, if using.
4 Tip in the spinach and cook for a couple of minutes.
5 Add about 100ml of water and continue to cook over a low heat for about 5–6 minutes.
6 Mix in the butter, followed by the paneer, and cook for 2 minutes.
7 Sprinkle with the coriander leaves and serve hot with chapatis or wholemeal pitta bread.

Purple Sprouting Broccoli with Onion and Mustard Seeds – Laal Broccoli ki Bhaji

Purple sprouting broccoli is more tender and sweeter than the more common green broccoli with its tightly packed florets. Before cooking, trim off any woody parts of the stems, divide into roughly evenly sized pieces, slice the thicker stems diagonally and rinse under cold water.

PREPARATION TIME: 10 MINUTES
COOKING TIME: 10 MINUTES
SERVES 4

pinch of salt plus ¼ tsp salt (optional)
pinch of sugar
400g purple sprouting broccoli, trimmed
2 tbsp olive oil
¼ tsp brown mustard seeds
1 onion, sliced
2 garlic cloves, chopped
¼ tsp turmeric
¼ tsp ground cumin
1 tsp lemon juice
pinch of freshly ground black pepper

1   Bring a pan of water to the boil over a high heat. Add the salt, sugar and the purple sprouting broccoli and cook for 2–3 minutes. Drain and set aside.
2   Heat a frying pan until hot and add the oil. Tip in the mustard seeds. When they start to sizzle, add the onion and garlic and fry for 3–4 minutes until the mixture is soft.
3   Add the turmeric, cumin and salt (if using) and stir-fry for 30 seconds before adding the drained broccoli. Stir-fry for 1 minute, then add the lemon juice and black pepper.
4   Serve with Chicken Reshmi Kebabs (page 44).

Spiced Peas – Sabut Mattar ki Sabzi

Peas are tiny powerhouses of nutrients, with high levels of antioxidants that boost the body's immune system. Many Indian main dishes include peas, but this recipe puts these nutritious vegetables centre stage. If you don't have mango powder, add a teaspoon of lemon juice just before serving.

PREPARATION TIME: 5 MINUTES
COOKING TIME: 8 MINUTES
SERVES 4

2 tbsp sunflower or olive oil
½ tsp brown or black mustard seeds
pinch of asafoetida
2 dried red chillies
½ tsp mango powder (amchur)
¼ tsp salt (optional)
500g frozen peas or petit pois, defrosted
a few washed and chopped coriander leaves

1 Heat the oil in a saucepan on a medium heat and sprinkle in a few of the mustard seeds; when they crackle, add the remaining seeds, the asafoetida and the chillies and stir for a minute.
2 Add the mango powder, salt, if using, and peas and stir for a further 4–5 minutes.
3 Add a couple of tablespoons of water and continue cooking for another minute.
4 Sprinkle with the coriander leaves and serve hot as a side dish.

Spiced Kale and Spinach – Desi Saag

Kale is a robust vegetable from the cabbage family; curly kale is the most popular variety. Select smallish heads of kale, which will be more tender, and remove the leaves from the tough stalks. *Saag* is a general term for leafy greens, and is also the name of a north Indian dish in which winter greens are cooked and seasoned with spices.

PREPARATION TIME: 20 MINUTES
COOKING TIME: 20 MINUTES
SERVES 4

200g curly kale leaves, washed thoroughly and roughly
    shredded or chopped
250g young spinach leaves, washed thoroughly
2 tbsp sunflower or rapeseed oil
1 onion, chopped
4 garlic cloves, chopped
2 green chillies, chopped
2 tsp peeled and grated fresh root ginger
1 tsp ground cumin
1 tsp ground coriander
½ tsp turmeric
¼ tsp salt (optional)
2 tsp tomato purée
generous knob of butter

1. Put the kale and the spinach in a large saucepan with about 120ml of cold water, bring to the boil and then simmer for 5–7 minutes.
2. Drain well, then place the greens in a blender and whizz until puréed. Set aside.
3. Heat a saucepan on a medium heat and add the oil. Add the onion, garlic and chillies and fry for 7–9 minutes until lightly browned.
4. Add the ginger, cumin, coriander, turmeric, salt, if using, tomato purée and butter and stir to combine. Mix in the puréed greens and cook for 2–3 minutes until well combined.
5. Serve hot with Indian Cheese with Toasted Fennel Seeds (page 30) and chapatis.

Tangy Aubergines – Kashmiri Khatte Baingan

This is a lighter take on a traditional dish from Kashmir that makes the most of aubergines (*brinjal* or *baingan*). Their deep purple colour comes from an antioxidant phytonutrient with the potential to lower cholesterol.

PREPARATION TIME: 10 MINUTES
COOKING TIME: 18 MINUTES
SERVES 4

400g baby aubergines, washed and tops removed
2 tbsp sunflower oil
pinch of asafoetida
¼ tsp cumin seeds
¼ tsp turmeric
generous pinch of chilli powder
¼ tsp salt (optional)
1 tsp lemon juice
1 tsp peeled and grated fresh root ginger
1 green chilli, finely chopped
pinch of garam masala
¼ tsp ground fennel seeds
a few mint leaves, washed and chopped

1 Slice each of the aubergines in half and set aside.
2 Heat a wok on a medium heat and add the oil. Add the asafoetida and the cumin seeds; when they start to crackle, add the aubergines and sauté for 10 minutes.
3 Mix in the turmeric, chilli powder and salt, if using, and cook for a further 5 minutes.
4 Sprinkle in the lemon juice, then the ginger and green chilli and mix. Add the garam masala and fennel, stir and cook for another minute.
5 Garnish with the mint leaves and serve with chapatis.

Light and Luscious Vegetable Curry

Fennel seeds, known as *saunf* in Hindi, can relieve bloating and stomach pains and they also serve as a mouth freshener when chewed after a meal. The fennel adds a slightly sweet edge to this sumptuous dish.

PREPARATION TIME: 5 MINUTES
COOKING TIME: 10 MINUTES
 SERVES 4

500g frozen mixed vegetables
2 tbsp natural yogurt
200g canned chopped tomatoes
1 tsp cumin seeds
2 tsp fennel seeds
2 tbsp sunflower or olive oil
½ tsp turmeric
1 tsp ground coriander
¼ tsp salt (optional)
1 tsp peeled and grated fresh root ginger
generous pinch of freshly ground black pepper

1 Boil the vegetables for 3–4 minutes. Drain and set aside.
2 Blend the yogurt with the tomatoes.
3 In a pestle and mortar, coarsely crush the cumin and fennel seeds.
4 Heat the oil in a heavy-based saucepan and tip in the seeds. When they begin to sizzle, add the turmeric, coriander and salt, if using. Mix for a minute, then add the vegetables and fry for 2 minutes.
5 Stir in the yogurt and tomato mixture and simmer for 2 minutes until droplets of oil appear on the surface. Stir in the ginger and black pepper. Serve with chapatis or wholemeal pitta breads and Mint Raita (page 152).

Cassava Curry – Mogo Curry

Cassava has almost twice as many calories as potatoes and sweet potatoes, but its natural sugars are released into the bloodstream at a slow, steady rate, thus avoiding blood sugar spikes that may contribute to weight gain. It also contains a good range of minerals necessary for the maintenance and functioning of the cells throughout the body.

PREPARATION TIME: 10 MINUTES
COOKING TIME: 45-50 MINUTES
SERVES 4

600g fresh or frozen cassava, peeled if fresh and chopped into chunks
3 tbsp olive or rapeseed oil
2cm piece of cinnamon stick
1 tsp cumin seeds
1 onion, finely chopped
4 garlic cloves, chopped
2 green chillies, finely chopped
½ tsp ground coriander
¼ tsp turmeric
¼ tsp chilli powder
¼ tsp salt (optional)
1 tsp tomato purée
300g passata or 400g canned chopped tomatoes, blended
1 tsp peeled and grated fresh root ginger
pinch of garam masala
a few washed and chopped coriander leaves

1   Boil the cassava in plenty of just-boiled water for 25 minutes until tender but not mushy. Drain and cut into 4cm pieces.
2   Heat a large saucepan on a medium heat and add the oil, then add the cinnamon and cumin seeds. When they begin to sizzle, add the onion and fry for 5–7 minutes until soft.
3   Add the garlic and fry for a minute, then mix in the chillies and fry for a further 2 minutes.
4   Add the ground coriander, turmeric, chilli powder and salt, if using, and mix well. Add the cassava pieces and cook for 3 minutes.
5   Stir in the tomato purée and the passata or blended tomatoes and cook for 5 minutes until droplets of oil appear on the surface.
6   Mix in the ginger and the garam masala and garnish with the coriander leaves. Serve hot with plain basmati rice.

Bengali Five Spice Vegetables – Panch Tarkari

Nigella seeds are one of the five spices in the Bengali five spice mixture known as *panch phoran* (see page 8). They are believed to possess many healing properties, from treating nasal congestion to relieving headaches, digestive disorders and arthritis. They are delicious and nutty and are used to flavour many vegetable and lentil dishes.

PREPARATION TIME: 15 MINUTES
COOKING TIME: 20 MINUTES
SERVES 4

1 tbsp rapeseed or olive oil
2 bay leaves
½ tsp brown or black mustard seeds
½ tsp fennel seeds
½ tsp nigella seeds
½ tsp cumin seeds
pinch of fenugreek seeds (optional)
200g potatoes, peeled and chopped into 1cm pieces
200g carrots, peeled and chopped into 1cm pieces
100g peas or petit pois, defrosted if frozen
200g cauliflower florets, cut into small pieces
1 green chilli, finely chopped
2 tsp peeled and grated fresh root ginger
½ tsp turmeric
¼ tsp salt (optional)
¼ tsp garam masala

1 Heat a pan on a medium heat and add the oil, then put in the bay leaves and a few mustard seeds; when they start to crackle, tip in the remaining mustard seeds, fennel, nigella, cumin and fenugreek seeds, if using. Give it a stir and then add the potatoes.

2 Sauté for 5 minutes and then mix in the carrots, peas or petit pois and cauliflower and cook for a couple of minutes.

3 Mix in the green chilli, ginger, turmeric and salt, if using. Pour in 100ml of just-boiled water, cover and cook for 8–10 minutes until the potatoes are tender.

4 Sprinkle over the garam masala and serve hot.

Rajasthani Okra – Rajasthani Bhindi

Okra – sometimes known as ladies' fingers or gumbo – contains high levels of mucilaginous fibre, which can help to reduce excess cholesterol. In India, okra is usually enjoyed in 'dry' dishes. This recipe from Rajasthan generally includes deep frying the okra, but I've adapted the method to sautéing, which uses far less oil.

PREPARATION TIME: 10 MINUTES
COOKING TIME: 10 MINUTES
SERVES 4

250g whole okra pods, washed
1 tbsp gram flour (besan)
1 tsp mango powder (amchur)
½ tsp turmeric
1½ tsp fennel seeds
4 tbsp sunflower oil
¼ tsp salt (optional)
4 green chillies, chopped
¼ tsp cumin seeds
½ tsp nigella seeds

1 Cut off the tops of the okra pods and cut a slit along one side of each pod.
2 Mix the gram flour with the mango powder and turmeric and ½ teaspoon of the fennel seeds. Add a tablespoon of the oil and the salt, if using. Mix well.
3 Using a teaspoon, place a small amount of the flour mixture into each okra pod.
4 Heat the remaining 3 tablespoons of oil in a frying pan and add the chillies, the remaining fennel seeds, the cumin seeds and nigella seeds. Fry for a minute.
5 Put the okra in the pan and fry for a couple of minutes. Cover the pan and cook on a low heat for 3–4 minutes.
6 Remove the cover and stir-fry until the okra pods are lightly browned on the outside. Serve hot with chapatis.

Runner Beans – Hara Sabzi

My mum grows runner beans in her garden and sometimes she just eats them raw, which is often the best way to reap the optimum nutritional benefits of certain vegetables. Top, tail and string runner beans by carefully sliding the knife into the top of the bean without cutting right through it; if a thick thread comes away, the beans will need to be stringed. Use runner beans as soon as possible after picking or buying. You can keep them in a paper bag in the fridge for 2–3 days.

PREPARATION TIME: 10 MINUTES
COOKING TIME: 15 MINUTES
SERVES 4

500g runner beans, washed, topped and tailed
3 tbsp sunflower or olive oil
¼ tsp brown or black mustard seeds
1 onion, finely chopped
1 tsp turmeric
1 tsp ground coriander
1 tsp paprika
¼ tsp salt (optional)

1   Run a potato peeler or knife down either side of the beans to remove any stringy bits. Cut on the diagonal into 2cm pieces.
2   Heat a frying pan on a medium heat, add the oil and add a few of the mustard seeds; when they crackle, add the remaining seeds. Mix for a minute then add the onion and fry for 5–7 minutes until lightly browned.
3   Tip in the beans and sauté for 2 minutes until they are coated with the onion mixture.
4   Add the turmeric, coriander, paprika and salt, if using. Mix well and cook for 1 minute.
5   Add about 5 tablespoons of water, cover the pan and simmer for 5 minutes until the beans are tender. Serve hot with a meat or chicken dish.

Sindhi Spinach – Sindhi Sai Bhaji

This dish originates from the province of Sindh in Pakistan. Spinach has many health benefits: it contains vitamins A, C and K, folate and various antioxidant phytonutrients such as beta-carotene. This combination of greens and protein-rich chana dal makes a delicious and nutritious meal.

PREPARATION TIME: 10 MINUTES, PLUS 20 MINUTES SOAKING
COOKING TIME: 50 MINUTES
SERVES 4

100g yellow split peas (chana dal or Bengal gram)
2 tbsp olive oil
1 onion, chopped
4–5 garlic cloves, chopped
1 green chilli, chopped
1 tsp peeled and grated fresh root ginger
½ tsp turmeric
1 tsp ground coriander
½ tsp ground cumin
¼ tsp chilli powder
¼ tsp salt (optional)
2 tomatoes, chopped
250g baby spinach leaves, washed
¼ tsp garam masala

1 Wash the chana dal and soak in 500ml of water for about 20 minutes.
2 Tip into a pressure cooker and cook for 10 minutes. Set aside. If you don't have a pressure cooker, place the chana dal in a saucepan with approximately 400ml of water and bring to the boil. Reduce the heat and boil gently for 35–40 minutes until the chana dal is soft but not mushy.
3 Heat a saucepan on a medium heat and add the oil. Add the onion, garlic and green chilli and sauté for 5–7 minutes until soft and lightly browned.
4 Add the ginger and stir in, then add the turmeric, coriander, cumin, chilli powder and salt, if using. Cook for a minute.
5 Mix in the tomatoes and cook for 2 minutes or until the mixture becomes thick.
6 Stir in the spinach leaves and cook for a minute until the spinach has slightly wilted. Add the cooked chana dal with its cooking water and simmer for 5–7 minutes until well combined.
7 Sprinkle in the garam masala. If you'd like a softer texture, you could use a potato masher or a hand-held blender to purée the mixture. Serve hot with plain basmati rice.

South Indian Brussels Sprouts

Brussels sprouts seem to divide opinion: people either love them or hate them. They look like miniature cabbages and like other members of the cabbage family they are packed with a unique combination of health-protecting antioxidants. Their nutty flavour makes them a good match for spices. The addition of curry leaves and coconut adds a touch of southern Indian flair to this dish.

PREPARATION TIME: 15 MINUTES
COOKING TIME: 18 MINUTES
SERVES 4

450g Brussels sprouts, trimmed and slit
3 tbsp sunflower or olive oil
2 tsp brown or black mustard seeds
½ tsp skinned split black lentils (urad dal)
6–8 curry leaves
1 onion, chopped
2–3 green chillies, slit lengthways
½ tsp turmeric
¼ tsp salt (optional)
2 tbsp unsweetened desiccated coconut

1   Place the Brussels sprouts into a saucepan of boiling water and cook for about 6 minutes until slightly soft but still with a bite. Drain them and set aside.

2   Heat a frying pan on a medium heat and add the oil. Add a few mustard seeds; when they start to splutter, add the remaining mustard seeds and lentils and stir for a minute.

3   Add the curry leaves and mix, then add the onion and green chillies and fry for 6–7 minutes until golden brown.

4   Add the turmeric and salt (if using), then tip in the sprouts and mix well. Cook for 2–3 minutes until the sprouts have picked up the flavours of the spices.

5   Sprinkle with the coconut and serve hot with chapatis.

Spiced Cauliflower – Gobhi Masala

Gobhi masala is a signature dish for many Asian households. Cauliflowers are closely related to broccoli, cabbage and kale: these vegetables are a good source of vitamin C and dietary fibre, and also contain a range of phytonutrient compounds with many health benefits. If you can get hold of purple cauliflowers, even better, as they contain an antioxidant called anthocyanin which may assist in regulating blood sugar levels.

PREPARATION TIME: 15 MINUTES
COOKING TIME: 25 MINUTES
SERVES 4

500g cauliflower florets, cut into 4cm pieces
3 tbsp olive oil
1 onion, finely chopped
2 green chillies, finely chopped
2–4 garlic cloves, finely chopped
1 tsp turmeric
½ tsp ground cumin
½ tsp ground coriander
generous pinch of freshly ground black pepper
¼ tsp salt (optional)
¼ tsp garam masala
2 ripe red tomatoes, coarsely chopped
1 tsp peeled and finely grated fresh root ginger

1 Wash the cauliflower in salted cold water. Drain well.
2 Heat the oil in a frying pan and lightly sauté the cauliflower florets for 5–6 minutes until they are slightly browned.
3 Remove the cauliflower from the pan and set aside. Add the onion, chillies and garlic, and fry for 7 minutes or until the onion is translucent.
4 Tip the cauliflower back into the pan and fry for a further 3 minutes until light brown. Add the turmeric, cumin, coriander, pepper, salt (if using) and garam masala, stir and fry gently for 5 minutes.
5 Meanwhile, purée the tomatoes until smooth. Add the tomatoes to the pan and cook for another 5 minutes.
6 Add 5 tablespoons of cold water, cover and simmer for 5 minutes. Stir in the ginger and serve hot.

Jerusalem Artichokes – Bharta

Bharta is a spiced mash, often made from roasted aubergines. Here, I've used Jerusalem artichokes, which have a delicate flavour and taste divine when roasted and mashed with a few spices. They're a great source of dietary fibre, but they can be quite heavy on the stomach so I've included asafoetida: it's a spice that suppresses that bloated feeling. This dish makes a great accompaniment to a chicken curry.

PREPARATION TIME: 20 MINUTES
COOKING TIME: 30 MINUTES
SERVES 4

500g Jerusalem artichokes, washed
3 tbsp sunflower or olive oil
¼ tsp asafoetida
1 tsp cumin seeds
2 onions, finely chopped
3 garlic cloves, crushed or finely chopped
2 tsp peeled and finely grated fresh root ginger
2 green chillies, finely chopped
2 tomatoes, finely chopped
1½ tsp ground coriander
½ tsp ground cumin
½ tsp garam masala
¼ tsp salt (optional)
2 tbsp washed and finely chopped coriander leaves

1 Preheat the oven to 180°C/gas mark 4.
2 Remove as much you can of the skin from the artichokes. Much like potatoes, the skin can be scrubbed clean or peeled off with a paring knife. Place the artichokes in a roasting tin and drizzle over 2 tablespoons of the oil, turning them over to coat them in oil. Roast in the centre of the oven for 20 minutes until they are lightly browned.
3 Heat a large frying pan on a medium heat and add the remaining oil. When hot, add the asafoetida and the cumin seeds and cook until the spluttering stops. Add the onions and sauté for 5–7 minutes until they are soft and translucent.
4 Add the garlic and ginger and fry for 1 minute, then mix in the green chillies.
5 Tip in the tomatoes and the ground coriander, cumin, garam masala and salt, if using. Stir well and cook for 3–5 minutes, stirring often to prevent the mixture from sticking to the pan. Sprinkle in a little water if needed.
6 Add the roasted artichokes and mix well, mashing them with a spoon as you mix. Add the coriander leaves and stir. Serve hot with chapatis.

Purple Cabbage with Toasted Gram Flour – Kobhi Zunka

Purple cabbage, also known as red cabbage, is packed with anthocyanins; these are antioxidant pigments that may lower the risk of heart disease and macular degeneration. Zunka is a western Indian dish made with gram flour. This flour is made from ground yellow split peas; it has more protein and fewer calories than wheat flour.

PREPARATION TIME: 10 MINUTES
COOKING TIME: 15 MINUTES
SERVES 4

2 tbsp gram flour (besan)
2 tbsp sunflower or olive oil
½ tsp brown or black mustard seeds
pinch of asafoetida
5–6 curry leaves (optional)
250g purple cabbage, washed and finely shredded
¼ tsp turmeric
¼ tsp ground coriander
¼ tsp chilli powder
¼ tsp salt (optional)

1   Heat a small heavy-based pan on a medium to low heat and
    add the gram flour. Toast it for 3–4 minutes, stirring to avoid
    lumps forming, until you can smell the aroma of the flour
    and the colour changes slightly. Remove from the heat and
    set aside.
2   Heat the oil in a large pan on a medium heat and add a few of
    the mustard seeds; when they crackle, add the remaining
    seeds. Add the asafoetida and curry leaves, if using, and stir.
3   Add the cabbage, turmeric, coriander, chilli powder and salt,
    if using. Mix well. Reduce the heat and sauté the cabbage for
    5–7 minutes until it is slightly soft and changes colour.
4   Add the toasted gram flour and stir well. It will absorb the
    liquid and oil to form clumps. Break them up as you cook for
    3 minutes more. Serve hot with chapatis.

Stuffed Bitter Gourds – Masaledaar Karela

Bitter gourd or bitter melon, known as *karela*, originated in India and is widely grown in Asia, Africa and the Caribbean. There are a number of varieties: the type most popular in India is about 10–15cm long, with a distinctive green jagged surface. They have many uses in traditional Indian medicine and though they are bitter in taste, many people in India drink the extracted juice, which you could make by putting the vegetables in a juicer. This dish is softened by the nutty sweetness of gram flour.

PREPARATION TIME: 15 MINUTES
COOKING TIME: 20-30 MINUTES
SERVES 2

4 bitter gourds or karelas, washed
1 tbsp rapeseed oil
1 onion, finely chopped
1 tsp ground cumin
1 tsp ground coriander
½ tsp turmeric
¼ tsp salt (optional)
2 tbsp gram flour (besan)
2 tsp lemon juice

1 Make a slit lengthways down the centre of each gourd. Remove and discard some of the seeds and set the gourds aside.
2 Heat the oil in a pan, add the onion and fry for 5–7 minutes until golden brown.
3 Add the cumin, coriander, turmeric and salt, if using, and mix for a minute. Add the gram flour and mix thoroughly for 2 minutes. Mix in the lemon juice.
4 Spoon the mixture into the bitter gourds, packing them tightly. Tie the gourds with string to ensure that the mixture does not spill out.
5 Place the bitter gourds in a steamer and steam for 15–20 minutes until tender. Serve hot with chapatis and Mint Raita (page 152).

CHAPTER 4

Lentils and Pulses

Pulses – the edible seeds of beans, peas and lentils – are also known as legumes and, in Hindi, as dals. In many Asian households, a dish of pulses is prepared at least once a day. They are a cheap and valuable source of protein and are used not only in main dishes, soups and stuffings, but also in puddings, and are milled to produce flours to make batter for pancakes. When preparing dried pulses, make sure that you soak them according to the instructions on the packet. Some carbohydrates that are present in pulses can be difficult to digest and may lead to a feeling of bloatedness; a pinch of asafoetida can help to reduce this.

Seasoned Lentils – Tarka Dal

Butter is a simple, natural product and contains vitamins A, D, E and K along with other compounds with health-promoting properties. However, it is a saturated fat and should be eaten in moderation. The butter provides the creaminess to this dish, which is a staple on many an Asian dinner table.

PREPARATION TIME: 5 MINUTES
COOKING TIME: 40 MINUTES
SERVES 4

200g split red lentils (masoor dal)
45g unsalted butter
pinch of asafoetida
6 curry leaves (optional)
1 green chilli, chopped, or 2 dried red chillies
1 onion, chopped
½ tsp ground cumin
½ tsp turmeric
¼ tsp salt (optional)

1   Put the lentils in a sieve and rinse under cold running water for about 30 seconds.
2   Bring 500ml of water to the boil in a large saucepan over a high heat. Add the lentils and bring the water back to the boil. Partially cover the pan, reduce the heat and simmer, stirring occasionally, for 20–30 minutes until the mixture becomes mushy. Top up with boiling water if necessary.
3   Melt the butter in a frying pan on a medium heat.
4   Add the asafoetida, curry leaves, if using, the green chilli or dried red chillies and stir for a few seconds. Then add the onion and fry for 5–7 minutes until soft.
5   Stir in the cumin, turmeric and salt, if using. Cook for a minute.
6   Add the onion mixture to the cooked lentils and cook for a further 2 minutes. Serve hot with chapatis.

Bengali-style Lentils – Bengali Dal Tarkari

Lentils contain high levels of soluble fibre, which can help to reduce cholesterol and keeps you feeling full for longer. They are also a good source of protein and contain virtually no fat. By combining them with spices you can create many flavoursome recipes, such as this Bengali-style dish using the east Indian five spice mixture known as *panch phoran*.

PREPARATION TIME: 10 MINUTES
COOKING TIME: 40 MINUTES
SERVES 4

200g split red lentils (masoor dal)
¼ tsp turmeric
2 tbsp olive oil or unsalted butter
pinch of asafoetida
¼ tsp panch phoran (page 8)
1 small onion or 2–3 shallots, sliced
1 green chilli, chopped
¼ tsp salt (optional)
1 tomato, chopped

1 Put the lentils in a sieve and rinse under cold running water for a few seconds. Then soak them in cold water for 5 minutes.
2 Drain the lentils and place in a saucepan with 400ml of boiling water and the turmeric and simmer gently for 25–30 minutes or until the lentils are tender.
3 In a separate pan, heat the oil or butter and add the asafoetida. When it crackles, add the panch phoran and stir for a few seconds until the seeds crackle.
4 Add the onion or shallots and fry for 5 minutes until soft.
5 Mix in the chilli and salt, if using, then add the tomato. Tip the spice mixture into the lentils and cook for a further 2 minutes. Serve hot with plain basmati rice.

Yellow Dal – Peeli Tarka Dal

Lentils, split peas and beans are a low-cost protein option and are relatively quick to prepare when compared to dried chickpeas and whole beans. Moong dal are skinned and split mung beans; they are yellow when the skins are removed. They don't hold their shape once cooked so are used in soups and puréed preparations. Tarka means seasoning and this simple recipe uses fresh green chillies and asafoetida as the seasoning.

PREPARATION TIME: 5 MINUTES
COOKING TIME: 20 MINUTES
SERVES 4

150g yellow split mung beans (moong dal)
2 tbsp olive or rapeseed oil
pinch of asafoetida
¼ tsp turmeric
2 green chillies, slit lengthways
¼ tsp salt (optional)

1   Rinse the moong dal in cold water, drain and place them in a saucepan with 450ml of cold water. Bring to the boil, using a slotted spoon to skim off any foam or scum that rises to the surface.
2   Reduce the heat, partially cover the pan and cook for 10–12 minutes until the dal start to split open and soften. Add a little hot water from the kettle if the consistency seems too thick. Remove from the heat and set aside.
3   In a frying pan, heat the oil and add the asafoetida, turmeric, chillies and salt, if using. Stir for a minute and then carefully pour the oily mixture into the lentils. Serve hot with wholemeal pitta breads or chapatis.

Brown Chickpeas with Onions – Kala Chana Pyaz

The inclusion of fibre-rich foods in your diet can greatly contribute to weight loss. Chickpeas contain both soluble and insoluble fibre, which are essential for maintaining the health of the digestive tract. The phytonutrients found in chickpeas also act as antioxidants that may help to prevent osteoporosis and can minimise hot flushes during the menopause. Chickpeas taste great in curries and are often used in festive dishes in India. Use 'kala chana' or brown chickpeas if you can find them.

PREPARATION TIME: 15 MINUTES
COOKING TIME: 15 MINUTES
SERVES 4

3 tbsp olive oil
1 onion, chopped
4 garlic cloves, chopped
4 green chillies, chopped
2 tsp peeled and grated fresh root ginger
½ tsp ground coriander
½ tsp ground cumin
¼ tsp salt (optional)
2 tbsp lemon juice
2 x 400g cans chickpeas, rinsed and drained
a few washed and chopped coriander leaves

1   Heat the oil in a large saucepan on a medium heat, then add the onion, garlic, chillies and ginger. Fry for 5–7 minutes until the onion is lightly browned.
2   Add the ground coriander, cumin and salt, if using, and mix well. Add the lemon juice, followed by the chickpeas, and cook for 3–4 minutes.
3   Then add about 4 tablespoons of water and cook for 2 minutes more.
4   Sprinkle over the coriander leaves and serve with wholemeal pitta breads or chapatis.

Lentils with Spinach – Dal Palak

If you're thinking of cutting down on meat, pulses are the perfect replacement, as they're rich in proteins, complex carbohydrates and fibre, and very low in fat. This nutritious dish is a popular vegetable delicacy, combining spinach with pulses and spices.

PREPARATION TIME: 15 MINUTES, PLUS 15 MINUTES SOAKING
COOKING TIME: 25 MINUTES
SERVES 4

200g yellow split mung beans (moong dal)
3–4 garlic cloves
1 tsp peeled and grated fresh root ginger
2 green chillies, roughly chopped
1 onion, roughly chopped
½ tsp chilli powder
½ tsp turmeric
1 tbsp ghee or unsalted butter
1 tsp cumin seeds
1 tomato, finely chopped
¼ tsp salt (optional)
250g baby spinach leaves, washed

1   Put the moong dal in a sieve and rinse under cold running
    water for a few seconds. Place them in a bowl, cover with
    cold water and leave to soak for 15 minutes.
2   Drain the soaked dal and place in a saucepan with 500ml of
    cold water. Bring to the boil, then cover and cook on a low
    heat for 20 minutes until tender.
3   Put the garlic, ginger, chillies and onion in a food processor
    and blend to a coarse paste. Mix in the chilli powder and
    turmeric and set aside.
4   Heat the ghee or butter in a saucepan on a medium heat and
    add a few of the cumin seeds; when they begin to crackle, add
    the remaining seeds and mix. Tip in the spice paste and
    sauté for a couple of minutes.
5   Stir in the tomato and salt, if using, and cook for 3 minutes
    until the mixture is well combined.
6   Add the cooked dal to the spice mixture and cook for
    2 minutes.
7   Add the spinach leaves and cook for a further 3 minutes.
    Serve hot with chapatis.

Kidney Beans Curry – Rajma Masala

Canned beans are convenient and an ideal time saver. However, they are quite different in flavour and texture from the dried beans cooked from scratch. If you plan to used dried beans, it's essential to soak them in water overnight. The complex sugars contained in beans cause bloatedness, and once the beans are soaked, the water begins to break down the complex sugars into simple ones that are easier to digest. Spiced kidney beans served with large plates of plain rice is a famous northern Indian dish sold during the winter months at roadside cafés.

PREPARATION TIME: 10 MINUTES,
PLUS OVERNIGHT SOAKING IF USING DRIED BEANS
COOKING TIME: 20 MINUTES,
PLUS 90 MINUTES BOILING IF USING DRIED BEANS
SERVES 4

2 x 400g cans kidney beans, drained, or 200g dried
  kidney beans
3 tbsp sunflower oil
2 onions, chopped
4–6 garlic cloves, sliced
1 tsp ground cumin
½ tsp ground coriander
½ tsp turmeric
½ tsp chilli powder
¼ tsp salt (optional)
1 tbsp tomato purée
½ tsp garam masala

1   If you're using kidney beans from a can, place them in a sieve
    and rinse under cold water for a few seconds; set aside.
2   If you're using dried kidney beans, rinse the beans and put
    them in a large bowl. Fill the bowl with cold water; there
    should be three times more water than beans (so, around
    600ml). Leave to soak overnight. The beans will absorb the
    water and double in size. Rinse and drain the beans three or
    four times until the water runs clear. Put the beans in a
    saucepan and add fresh cold water to come about 3cm above
    the beans. Bring to the boil. Using a slotted spoon, skim off
    any froth that rises to the surface. Reduce the heat, cover the
    pan and simmer for at least 1 hour 15 minutes or until the
    beans are soft.
3   Heat a large frying pan and add the oil, then add the onions
    and garlic and fry for 7–9 minutes until the onions are
    caramelised.
4   Add the cumin, coriander, turmeric, chilli powder and salt, if
    using. Mix well then stir in the tomato purée.
5   Tip in the kidney beans with their liquid (if cooked from
    dried beans). If you're using canned beans, add 250ml of
    water. Cook for 5 minutes.
6   Sprinkle over the garam masala. Serve hot with plain
    basmati rice.

Spiced Black Lentils – Halka Dal Makhani

Also known as *sabut urad*, these black lentils are a rich source of protein and dietary fibre, B vitamins and many minerals. They are used extensively in Indian cooking as an ingredient for poppadoms and the south Indian pancakes known as *dosa*. This preparation is popular in northern India and beyond, where the lentils are slow cooked for hours to create a rich, indulgent stew laced with lots of butter and more often than not cream. This recipe also includes kidney beans: you can use drained canned kidney beans or beans you have cooked from scratch.

PREPARATION TIME: 15 MINUTES, PLUS 8 HOURS SOAKING
COOKING TIME: 55 MINUTES
SERVES 4

115g whole black lentils (urad dal)
3 tbsp sunflower oil
pinch of asafoetida
1 onion, finely chopped
2 green chillies, finely chopped
3–4 garlic cloves, chopped
¼ tsp salt (optional)
½ tsp turmeric
1 tsp ground coriander
1 tsp ground cumin
115g cooked kidney beans, rinsed
2 tsp peeled and finely grated fresh root ginger
¼ tsp garam masala
2 tbsp single cream
a few washed and chopped coriander leaves

1   Check through the black lentils and pick out any stones. Place in a sieve and rinse the lentils under cold running water. Soak them in cold water for 8 hours or overnight.

2   Rinse them and place in a saucepan with 400ml of just-boiled water. Bring to the boil, then cover and simmer for 30 minutes until the lentils are tender. Set aside with the cooking water in the pan.

3   Heat a large frying pan on a medium heat and add the oil, then mix in the asafoetida and the onion, chillies and garlic and fry for 7–8 minutes until lightly browned.

4   Add the salt, if using, turmeric, ground coriander and cumin. Stir well to combine the spices.

5   Add the kidney beans and the black lentils along with the water in which the lentils were cooked. Mix and cook for a couple of minutes.

6   Add the ginger and 400ml of just-boiled water and simmer for 10 minutes.

7   Sprinkle over the garam masala and swirl in the cream. Garnish with the coriander leaves. Serve hot with plain basmati rice.

Punjabi Chickpeas – Pindi Chole

Chickpeas provide a vegetarian source of protein and a rich source of dietary fibre. Northern Indians relish the flavour of chickpeas and love to create tangy or richly spiced dishes for everyday eating as well as for special occasions.

PREPARATION TIME: 10 MINUTES
COOKING TIME: 30 MINUTES
SERVES 4

3 tbsp olive or sunflower oil
pinch of asafoetida
2 onions, chopped
4 tomatoes, chopped, or 400g canned chopped tomatoes
½ tsp turmeric
¼ tsp salt (optional)
1½ tbsp chana masala spice blend (page 11)
400g can chickpeas, rinsed and drained
3cm piece of fresh root ginger, peeled, then chopped
    into thin strips

1   Heat a large pan on a medium heat and add the oil, then mix in the asafoetida and the onions and fry for 7–8 minutes until golden brown.
2   Add the tomatoes and fry for 5 minutes until the mixture is quite thick.
3   Add the turmeric and salt, if using, and mix well, then add the chana masala spice blend, mix well and cook for a minute.
4   Add the chickpeas and cook, stirring, for about 5 minutes until the mixture is well combined.
5   Pour in 250ml of just-boiled water and leave to simmer for 6–7 minutes until the mixture becomes quite thick. Serve hot with chapatis.

....

CHAPTER 5

Chicken

When preparing dishes based on meat or poultry, it is important to balance the protein intake with plenty of vegetable side dishes. Chicken has less saturated fat than beef, lamb or pork, and removing the skin reduces the fat content even further, as well as allowing the spices to penetrate the chicken. Many Indian chicken dishes are prepared with rich sauces; in this chapter I've created spiced sauces with a lower oil content. In the West, one dish that's synonymous with Indian cuisine is tandoori chicken. It is customarily baked in a clay oven and is a healthy option in restaurants that present it with a salad and chutney.

Tandoori Chicken – Tandoori Murgh

The traditional way to make tandoori chicken is by marinating the meat with spices and yogurt and then cooking it in a *tandoor* – a clay oven heated by charcoal. It is one of the healthiest ways of eating chicken as it is not served with a rich sauce. These days, very few Indian households have a *tandoor* but roasting in a hot oven will provide similar results.

PREPARATION TIME: 15 MINUTES, PLUS 35 MINUTES MARINATING
COOKING TIME: 45 MINUTES
SERVES 4

800g skinless and boneless chicken thighs
4 tbsp lemon juice
2 tbsp peeled and grated fresh root ginger
6–8 garlic cloves, crushed
½ tsp Kashmiri chilli powder
¼ tsp salt
400ml natural yogurt, whisked
1 tbsp garam masala
2 tbsp sunflower or olive oil
1 tbsp dried fenugreek leaves (kasoori methi) (optional)
1 tbsp melted butter
2 red onions, chopped into rings
1 lemon, cut into wedges

1. Using a sharp knife, make two or three incisions in the chicken pieces.
2. In a bowl large enough to hold the chicken, mix the lemon juice, 1 tablespoon of the ginger, half of the crushed garlic and the Kashmiri chilli powder. Add the chicken pieces and coat evenly with the spice mixture. Cover and place in the fridge for 20 minutes.
3. Mix together the yogurt, the remaining 1 tablespoon of ginger, the remaining garlic, the garam masala, oil and fenugreek, if using.
4. Remove the chicken from the fridge and add the yogurt marinade. Coat the chicken well. Cover the bowl and return to the fridge for a further 15 minutes.
5. Preheat the oven to 200°C/gas mark 6. Place the chicken pieces in a roasting tin with the marinade and cover with foil. Place in the oven for 20 minutes.
6. Baste with the melted butter and cook for a further 20–25 minutes, until the juices run clear when a skewer is inserted into the chicken.
7. Serve hot with red onion rings and lemon wedges and Mint Raita (page 152).

Quick Chicken Curry

Everyone has their favourite chicken curry, but sometimes it's refreshing to try something different. I use yogurt to finish this dish, which adds a creamy texture. Natural yogurt contains beneficial bacteria that promote the health of the digestive tract, as well as calcium, which helps to maintain bone density.

PREPARATION TIME: 10 MINUTES
COOKING TIME: 18 MINUTES
SERVES 4

2 tbsp sunflower or olive oil
1 onion, finely chopped
3–4 garlic cloves, finely chopped or crushed
1 green chilli, finely chopped (optional)
4 skinless and boneless chicken breasts, cut into
    bite-sized pieces
1 tsp ground coriander
1 tsp ground cumin
½ tsp turmeric
pinch of chilli powder
¼ tsp salt (optional)
2 tsp tomato purée
1 tsp peeled and grated fresh root ginger
generous pinch of garam masala
3 tbsp natural yogurt
a few washed and chopped coriander leaves

1 Heat a large saucepan or a wok on a medium heat then add the oil. Tip in the onion and cook, stirring frequently, for 5 minutes until the onion is soft.

2 Add the garlic and cook for 2 minutes until the mixture turns golden brown.

3 Add the green chilli, if using, and mix. Tip in the chicken pieces, reduce the heat to low and cook, stirring occasionally, for 6–7 minutes until the pieces turn white.

4 Add the ground coriander, cumin, turmeric, chilli powder and salt (if using), and fry for 1 minute.

5 Stir in the tomato purée, then add 150ml of water and simmer uncovered for 3 minutes, or until the chicken is cooked through. Check by cutting a piece of chicken in half; if it is white on the inside, it is cooked.

6 Mix in the ginger and garam masala. Stir in the yogurt until well combined. Garnish with the coriander leaves and serve hot with plain basmati rice.

Chettinad Chicken

This dish has all the flavours of a rich, luxurious curry but uses very little oil. Black peppercorns stimulate digestion and are said to be carminative, meaning that they help prevent the formation of intestinal gas. It is from the south Indian state of Tamil Nadu, where most dishes are eaten with rice.

PREPARATION TIME: 10 MINUTES, PLUS 10 MINUTES MARINATING
COOKING TIME: 25 MINUTES
SERVES 4

500g skinless and boneless chicken pieces, cut into
    2cm pieces
2 tbsp olive oil
2.5cm piece of cinnamon stick
4 green cardamoms
2 cloves
1 onion, chopped
6–8 curry leaves (optional)
2 tomatoes, chopped
½ tsp turmeric
a few washed and chopped coriander leaves

For the spice paste
2 dried red chillies, stalks removed
½ tsp black peppercorns
1 tsp fennel seeds
½ tsp cumin seeds
2 tsp peeled and grated fresh root ginger
4–6 garlic cloves, crushed
2 tbsp unsweetened desiccated or frozen grated coconut

1   First, make the spice paste: heat a pan on a medium heat. Add the red chillies, peppercorns, fennel and cumin seeds and roast for a couple of minutes. Remove from the heat and leave to cool.

2   Transfer them to a spice mill or a coffee grinder and grind to a medium to fine powder. Add the ginger, garlic and coconut and grind to a paste.

3   Place the chicken pieces in a bowl, add the spice paste and mix well. Cover and place in the fridge for 10 minutes.

4   Heat the oil in a large saucepan on a medium heat and add the cinnamon, cardamoms and cloves. Stir for 30 seconds until the spices release their aromas.

5   Add the onion and the curry leaves, if using, and fry for 5–7 minutes until the onion is golden brown.

6   Add the tomatoes and sauté for 5 minutes.

7   Add the marinated chicken and turmeric and sauté for 10 minutes, adding 4 tablespoons of water.

8   Cover with a lid and cook on a medium to low heat until the chicken is cooked. Check by cutting a piece of chicken in half; if it is white on the inside, it is cooked.

9   Garnish with coriander leaves and serve with plain basmati rice.

Chicken Bharta

Bharta means mash in Hindi and this is an interesting way to serve lean chicken, with a richly infused spicy onion and cashew nut mash. Dried fenugreek leaves aid digestion.

PREPARATION TIME: 10 MINUTES
COOKING TIME: 30 MINUTES
SERVES 6

3 tbsp olive or rapeseed oil

1 tsp cumin seeds

3 onions, finely chopped

6 garlic cloves, finely chopped or crushed

2 green chillies, finely chopped

1kg skinless and boneless chicken breasts, chopped into 2cm pieces

½ tsp turmeric

¼ tsp chilli powder or Kashmiri chilli powder

¼ tsp salt (optional)

2 tsp tomato purée

20–25 unsalted cashew nuts, ground (optional)

2 tsp peeled and grated fresh root ginger

¼ tsp garam masala

2 tsp dried fenugreek leaves (kasoori methi)

a few washed and chopped coriander leaves

1   Heat a large pan on a medium heat and add the oil, then add
    the cumin seeds and sauté for a minute. Add the onions,
    garlic and chillies and fry for 10–12 minutes until the onions
    are golden brown.
2   Add the chicken pieces and sauté for 10–15 minutes until the
    chicken turns white.
3   Add the turmeric, chilli powder and salt, if using. Mix well
    for a minute.
4   Add the tomato purée and continue cooking for a couple of
    minutes.
5   Mix in the cashew nuts, if using, and cook for a further
    minute.
6   Add the ginger and garam masala and mix. Sprinkle in the
    fenugreek leaves and stir. Garnish with the coriander leaves
    and serve with chapatis.

Chicken Curry in Tomato Gravy

This is a fabulously flavoured tangy curry which is packed with spice. You can start the preparation of this sauce at the weekend and store it in the fridge to use with the chicken during the week.

PREPARATION TIME: 15 MINUTES
COOKING TIME: 25 MINUTES
SERVES 4

4 medium tomatoes
4–6 garlic cloves, roughly chopped
2 green chillies, roughly chopped
2cm piece of fresh root ginger, peeled and roughly chopped
2 tbsp rapeseed oil
4 skinless and boneless chicken breasts, chopped into
    2cm pieces
½ tsp ground coriander
½ tsp ground cumin
¼ tsp turmeric
pinch of salt
pinch of garam masala (optional)
a few washed and chopped coriander leaves

1   Using a knife, score an 'X' on the tomatoes and immerse
    them in a bowl of just-boiled water for about a minute.
    Remove from the water, peel off the skin and discard. Place
    the tomatoes in a food processor along with the garlic,
    chillies and ginger and blend until almost smooth.
2   Heat the oil in a non-stick frying pan on a medium heat and
    add the chicken. Fry for 10 minutes until lightly browned.
    Remove the chicken from the pan and set aside.
3   Add the blended sauce to the pan and cook for a minute. Add
    the ground coriander, cumin, turmeric and salt and cook for
    another minute.
4   Return the chicken to the pan and cook for a further
    2 minutes.
5   Swirl 150ml of water in the blender and pour into the pan.
    Simmer for 5–6 minutes.
6   Sprinkle with the garam masala, if using, and garnish with
    coriander leaves. Serve hot with plain basmati rice.

Chicken Vindaloo

This dish comes from the region of Goa, and includes both dried red chillies and chilli powder. Chillies are high in vitamin C and other compounds that act as powerful antioxidants to protect health. You could replace the chilli powder with a teaspoon of lemon juice to make a less spicy curry.

**PREPARATION TIME: 15 MINUTES,
PLUS AT LEAST 2 HOURS MARINATING
COOKING TIME: 20 MINUTES
SERVES 4**

10 black peppercorns
6 cloves
4 green cardamoms
1 tsp cumin seeds
1 tsp brown or black mustard seeds
5cm piece of fresh root ginger, peeled and coarsely chopped
6 garlic cloves
1 onion, roughly chopped
2 dried red chillies, chopped
½ tsp turmeric
½ tsp ground cinnamon
¼ tsp chilli powder (optional)
2 tbsp malt vinegar
1 tsp tomato purée
500g skinless and boneless chicken breasts, cut into
    bite-sized pieces
3 tbsp groundnut oil

1   Heat a frying pan on a medium heat. Add the peppercorns,
    cloves, cardamoms, cumin and mustard seeds and roast,
    shaking the pan occasionally, until you can smell the aroma
    of the spices. Watch carefully so they do not burn. Tip the
    spices on to a plate and leave to cool completely. Transfer to
    a spice mill or coffee grinder and grind to a medium to
    coarse powder.
2   Put the ginger, garlic, onion, dried chillies, turmeric,
    cinnamon, chilli powder, if using, vinegar and tomato purée
    into a blender, add the ground spice mixture and blend to a
    coarse, thick paste.
3   Put the chicken in a large non-metallic bowl, add the spice
    paste and mix thoroughly. Cover the bowl with cling film and
    place in the fridge for at least 2 hours or overnight.
4   Heat the oil in a large saucepan with a tight-fitting lid. Add
    the chicken and fry for 10 minutes, or until all the pieces are
    lightly browned. Meanwhile, bring 375ml water to the boil.
5   Pour the boiling water into the saucepan and bring back to
    the boil. Reduce the heat, cover and simmer for 15–20
    minutes until the chicken is tender. Serve hot with plain
    basmati rice.

Ginger Chicken – Lucknowi Adraki Murgh

Many people find that ginger can prevent or reduce motion sickness. It also contains potent anti-inflammatory compounds and many people who suffer from arthritis have reported a reduction in pain levels and improvements in their mobility when they consume ginger regularly.

PREPARATION TIME: 15 MINUTES
COOKING TIME: 25 MINUTES
SERVES 4

2 tbsp sunflower oil
2 onions, finely chopped
2–3 garlic cloves, chopped or crushed
2 green chillies, finely chopped
4 skinless and boneless chicken breasts, chopped into
   2cm pieces
1 tsp ground coriander
1 tsp ground cumin
1/2 tsp turmeric
1/2 tsp paprika (degi mirch)
1/4 tsp salt (optional)
1/4 tsp chilli powder (optional)
2 tsp tomato purée
generous pinch of garam masala
1 tbsp peeled and grated fresh root ginger
1/2 tsp dried fenugreek leaves (kasoori methi)
a few washed and chopped coriander leaves

1 Heat the oil in a large frying pan on a medium heat, add the onions and fry for 5–7 minutes until soft.
2 Add the garlic and chillies and continue frying for a further 2 minutes.
3 Mix in the chicken and cook for 5 minutes until the chicken turns white.
4 Add the ground coriander, cumin, turmeric, paprika, salt (if using) and chilli powder, if using. Mix well for a minute then add the tomato purée.
5 Pour in 125ml of just-boiled water and simmer for 3–5 minutes until droplets of oil appear on the surface.
6 Add the garam masala and the ginger and cook for a further minute.
7 Mix in the fenugreek leaves and scatter over the coriander leaves. Serve hot with chapatis or toasted wholemeal naan bread.

Malabar Chicken Curry

This is a popular dish from Kerala in southern India. It's a deliciously aromatic curry cooked in a spicy coconut gravy.

PREPARATION TIME: 15 MINUTES
COOKING TIME: 25 MINUTES
SERVES 4

2 tbsp olive or rapeseed oil
4–6 shallots, chopped
500g skinless and boneless chicken breasts, cut into
   2cm pieces
1 tbsp ground coriander
1/2 tsp turmeric
1/2 tsp chilli powder
1/4 tsp salt (optional)

For the spice paste
2.5cm piece of cinnamon stick or cassia bark
2 bay leaves
2 cloves
4 black peppercorns
500g unsweetened desiccated or freshly grated coconut
2.5cm piece of fresh root ginger, peeled and roughly chopped
4 garlic cloves, roughly chopped

For tempering
1 tsp olive or rapeseed oil
1/2 tsp brown or black mustard seeds
2 green chillies, slit lengthways

1   First, make the spice paste. Heat a frying pan on a medium heat and add the cinnamon or cassia, bay leaves, cloves and peppercorns. Roast and toss them gently for about a minute until you can smell the aroma of the spices. Tip the spices on to a plate and leave to cool. Transfer to a spice mill or blender and grind to a medium to fine powder.

2   Add the coconut, ginger and garlic and blend to a thick paste. Add 200ml of water and mix.

3   Heat the oil in a large frying pan, add the shallots and fry until soft.

4   Add the chicken and cook for 5 minutes until the chicken turns white.

5   Add the ground coriander, turmeric, chilli powder and salt (if using). Mix well and add the spice paste. Add 400ml of just-boiled water and cook for 10 minutes until the chicken is cooked through.

6   For tempering, heat a small frying pan and add the oil. Add a few of the mustard seeds; when they start to crackle, add the remaining seeds, followed by the chillies. Fry for a minute. Pour the mixture over the chicken curry and cook for a further 3 minutes.

7   Serve hot with plain basmati rice.

Punjabi Green Chicken Curry – Punjabi Haryali Murgh

This dish comes from Punjab in northern India where the cuisine is hearty and robust with lots of fresh greens. Nutrient-rich spinach is a good source of dietary fibre and vitamins A and K; the best way to reap all the benefits of spinach is by cooking lightly.

PREPARATION TIME: 15 MINUTES, PLUS 20 MINUTES MARINATING
COOKING TIME: 25 MINUTES
SERVES 4

6 tbsp natural yogurt
¼ tsp salt (optional)
1 tsp peeled and grated fresh root ginger
4–5 garlic cloves, crushed
½ tsp chilli powder
450g skinless and boneless chicken breasts, chopped into 2cm pieces
2 tbsp sunflower oil
400g canned chopped tomatoes, blended
8–10 unsalted cashew nuts, ground
generous pinch of garam masala
250g baby spinach leaves, washed
2 green chillies
10–12 mint leaves, washed
handful of coriander leaves, washed
¼ tsp turmeric
2 tsp ground coriander
½ tsp lemon juice
1 tsp unsalted butter
125ml single cream

1   In a bowl, mix the yogurt, salt (if using), ginger, garlic and
    ¼ teaspoon of the chilli powder. Add the chicken pieces and
    mix well. Cover and place in the fridge for 20 minutes.

2   Heat the oil in a saucepan on a medium heat and add the
    marinated chicken along with the marinade; cook for 5
    minutes until the chicken turns white on the outside.

3   Add the blended tomatoes and cashew nuts and stir in the
    garam masala. Cook for 10 minutes.

4   Meanwhile, put the spinach leaves, green chillies, mint and
    coriander leaves in a blender and blend to a fine paste.

5   Add the green paste to the pan with the chicken, then add the
    remaining chilli powder and the turmeric and mix well.
    Continue to cook for about 2–3 minutes on a low heat.

6   Add the ground coriander and cook for a couple of minutes
    until the sauce thickens.

7   Add the lemon juice and the butter, cover the pan and leave it
    for 2 minutes.

8   Finally, add the cream and mix well. Serve hot with plain
    basmati rice.

Griddled Chicken – Tawa Murgh

On the streets of Delhi, tawa chicken is cooked on a black griddle plate. It's quick to make as long as you chop the chicken into small pieces.

PREPARATION TIME: 15 MINUTES
COOKING TIME: 15 MINUTES
SERVES 4

2 tbsp olive or sunflower oil
4 skinless and boneless chicken breasts, chopped
  into 2cm pieces
2 tsp peeled and grated fresh root ginger
4–6 garlic cloves, crushed
½–1 tsp chilli powder
1 tsp ground coriander
¼ tsp turmeric
¼ tsp salt (optional)
2 tsp low-sodium soy sauce
1 red onion, sliced
4 lemon wedges

1   Heat the oil in a wok or a non-stick frying pan on a medium heat and add the chicken. Sauté for 8–10 minutes until the chicken turns white.
2   Add the ginger and garlic and stir-fry for 2–3 minutes until well combined.
3   Add the chilli powder, coriander, turmeric and salt, if using. Stir-fry for another minute and then sprinkle in the soy sauce.
4   Check that the chicken is cooked through by cutting a piece in half; if it is white on the inside, the chicken is cooked.
5   Serve hot with red onion slices and lemon wedges.

CHAPTER 6

Fish and Seafood

Much of India is surrounded by sea, which means there is a vast selection of fish and seafood dishes with many regional differences. In some parts of India, fish and rice is the staple diet. Coconut has a natural affinity with fish and seafood; several of the recipes in this chapter use coconut milk or fresh or frozen grated coconut.

A healthy diet should include at least two portions of fish or seafood a week, including one portion of oily fish such as salmon, mackerel or sardines. Fish provides a great range of nutrients and oily fish are particularly rich in omega-3 fatty acids, which are essential for good health and may help to protect your heart. Occasionally replacing red meat with fish will also reduce your saturated fat intake.

Fish in Tomato Curry

This fish preparation is traditionally made in the south of India with seerfish, an oily fish from the mackerel family, while in east India it is cooked using rohu, from the carp family. I've also made it with fillets of basa (sometimes known as river cobbler).

PREPARATION TIME: 10 MINUTES
COOKING TIME: 15 MINUTES
SERVES 4

2 tbsp ghee or butter
1 tsp cumin seeds
750g white fish fillets, cut into 4cm pieces
2 onions, finely chopped
6–8 garlic cloves, crushed
1 tsp turmeric
pinch of chilli powder
2 tsp tomato purée
2 tsp peeled and grated fresh root ginger
1 tsp garam masala

1 Heat a pan on a medium heat and add the ghee. Add a few of the cumin seeds; when they start to crackle, tip in the remaining seeds. Put the fish in the pan and sauté for 3–4 minutes until the fish begins to turn opaque. Remove from the pan and set aside.
2 Add the onions and sauté for 3 minutes until soft.
3 Add the garlic and fry for another minute. Mix in the turmeric and chilli powder, then add the tomato purée and 80ml of water, mix well and cook for 2 minutes.
4 Return the fish to the pan and simmer for about 3 minutes.
5 Stir in the ginger and sprinkle with the garam masala. Serve hot with chapatis.

Fish in Light Coconut Curry

Mustard seeds are a good source of selenium, which has anti-inflammatory properties and may help to relieve some of the symptoms associated with rheumatoid arthritis; they are also rich in magnesium, which is believed to reduce the incidence of migraine attacks. Mustard seeds also add a nutty flavour to curries and snacks.

PREPARATION TIME: 10 MINUTES
COOKING TIME: 15 MINUTES
SERVES 4

2 tbsp groundnut oil
1 tsp brown or black mustard seeds
1 onion, chopped
4 garlic cloves, chopped
2 green chillies, chopped
½ tsp turmeric
1 tsp ground coriander
¼ tsp salt (optional)
4 tbsp coconut milk
800g white fish fillets, cut into 4cm wide pieces

1   Heat the oil in a pan on a medium heat. Add a few of the mustard seeds; when they start to crackle, add the remaining seeds and stir. Add the onion and fry for 4–5 minutes until translucent.
2   Mix in the garlic and chillies and fry for a minute. Then add the turmeric, ground coriander and salt, if using, and mix well. Add 2 tablespoons of the coconut milk along with 100ml of water and mix. Put the fish pieces into the pan and simmer for 5–6 minutes.
3   Mix in the remaining 2 tablespoons of coconut milk and cook for another minute. Serve hot with plain basmati rice.

Green Masala Fish – Hara Masala Macchi

This is a version of the traditional Indian aromatic fish dish that is cooked in banana leaves: I've used foil instead of leaves. White fish is a good source of low-fat protein as well as B vitamins and iodine, which is vital for healthy metabolism.

PREPARATION TIME: 10 MINUTES
COOKING TIME: 30 MINUTES
SERVES 4

4cm piece of fresh root ginger, peeled and coarsely chopped
4–6 garlic cloves, crushed
2 tbsp olive oil, plus extra for brushing
½ tsp brown or black mustard seeds
½ tsp turmeric
80g washed and coarsely chopped coriander leaves
juice of 1 lemon
¼ tsp salt (optional)
¼ tsp coarsely ground black pepper
750–800g white fish fillets, such as pollack, coley or cod

1 Preheat the oven to 180°C/gas mark 4.

2 Place the ginger and garlic in a blender with 2 tablespoons of water and grind to a paste.

3 Heat the oil in a pan on a medium heat and add a few of the mustard seeds; when they crackle, add the remaining seeds and stir. Tip in the ginger and garlic paste along with the turmeric and stir-fry for a minute. Leave the mixture to cool.

4 Transfer this mixture to the blender with the coriander leaves, lemon juice, salt, if using, and the black pepper. Blend to a paste. Add a tablespoon of water if the mixture is too thick.

5 Line a baking tray with a large sheet of foil, allowing plenty to wrap around the fish, and brush the foil lightly with oil.

6 Put the fish in a bowl, add the spice paste and mix well.

7 Place fish on the foil and fold the foil over to seal the fish; the foil should not touch the top of the fish. Cook for 20–25 minutes until the fish is slightly firm and flaky.

8 Transfer to a serving platter, spooning any of the paste left on the foil on to the fish. Serve hot with plain basmati rice and a vegetable dish.

Fish with Peppers – Macchi Jalfrezi

Mangoes which are still unripe and green are peeled, sliced and then dried in the sun. They are then ground into a powder, known as *amchur* in Hindi. Mango powder is rich in vitamin C, and aids digestion. This spice imparts a sour fruity note and works well in dry fish dishes such as this light stir-fry.

PREPARATION TIME: 15 MINUTES
COOKING TIME: 20 MINUTES
SERVES 4

2 tsp ground coriander
1 tsp ground cumin
1 tsp mango powder (amchur)
½ tsp chilli powder
2 tsp peeled and grated fresh root ginger
500g white fish fillets, such as pollack, coley or cod,
    cut into 3cm pieces
2 tbsp sunflower oil
1 onion, cut into 2cm pieces
3 tbsp cornflour
1 red, 1 yellow and 1 green pepper, cut into 2cm pieces
1 tomato, chopped
a few washed and chopped coriander leaves

1. In a small bowl, mix the ground coriander, cumin, mango powder, chilli powder and ginger together.
2. Coat the fish with the spice mixture and set aside for 10 minutes.
3. Heat a frying pan on a medium heat and add 1 tablespoon of the oil. Add the onion and fry for 5 minutes until translucent. Remove from the pan and set aside.
4. Put the cornflour in a shallow dish and add the fish, turning it to coat it in the cornflour.
5. Add the remaining 1 tablespoon of oil to the pan on a low heat. Add the fish and cook for 5–7 minutes until lightly golden. Remove the fish and set aside.
6. Turn up the heat, add the peppers to the pan and stir-fry for 2 minutes. Mix in the onion and the fish and toss gently.
7. Garnish with the tomato and coriander leaves. Serve hot with chapatis.

Hot and Sour Fish Curry

Tamarind is a deliciously sweet and sour fruit that is a good source of iron. A healthy supply of iron ensures a proper red blood cell count. Turmeric is a spice that not only gives curries that distinctive yellow colour but also has powerful anti-inflammatory effects. Black pepper enhances the absorption of the healing compound curcumin, found in turmeric.

PREPARATION TIME: 10 MINUTES, PLUS 10 MINUTES SOAKING
COOKING TIME: 20 MINUTES
SERVES 4

2 tbsp tamarind pulp
800g white fish fillets, such as pollack, coley or cod
½ tsp turmeric
1 tbsp sunflower or olive oil
5–6 curry leaves (optional)
1 onion, chopped
½ tsp chilli powder
2 tsp ground coriander
½ tsp freshly ground black pepper
¼ tsp salt (optional)

1. Put the tamarind in a small bowl, pour in enough boiling water to cover and leave to stand for 10 minutes.
2. Using a wooden spoon, press the pulp to release the seeds and fibres, then strain through a nylon sieve into a bowl, pressing with the back of the spoon to extract as much juice as possible. Discard the pulp.
3. Rub the fish with the turmeric.
4. Heat the oil in a pan on a medium heat and add the curry leaves, if using, and mix well. Add the onion and fry for 5–7 minutes until lightly browned.
5. Add the chilli powder, ground coriander and black pepper and cook for a minute. Add 150ml water and cook on a low heat for 3 minutes.
6. Add the fish and the salt, if using, and mix carefully. Simmer for a further 3 minutes.
7. Pour in the tamarind juice and simmer for a couple more minutes until the fish is firm and white. Serve hot with plain basmati rice.

Fish in Mustard Sauce – Shorshe Maach

The kiosks along Decker's Lane in Kolkata's business district are the ultimate destination for lovers of street food. Among other things, you'll find a variety of fish dishes using locally caught fish prepared in an Indian 'fish and chip' style – with added spice. This recipe has a rich coconut sauce and includes two of Bengal's favourite ingredients – poppy seeds and mustard seeds.

PREPARATION TIME: 10 MINUTES
COOKING TIME: 20 MINUTES
SERVES 4

¼ tsp salt (optional)
500g white fish fillets such as hoki, pollack or haddock,
    cut into 4cm pieces
1 tbsp poppy seeds
3 tbsp rapeseed oil
2 tsp yellow mustard seeds
½ tsp turmeric
100g fresh or frozen grated coconut
1 tsp peeled and grated fresh root ginger
4 garlic cloves
1 green chilli
1 onion, roughly chopped
1 tsp ground coriander
1 tsp ground cumin
½ tsp chilli powder
juice of ½ a lemon

1. Sprinkle the salt, if using, over the fish and set aside.
2. Heat a frying pan on a medium heat, add the poppy seeds and toast them for a couple of minutes. Tip the seeds into a small bowl and add 3 tablespoons of water to cover them. Set aside for about 15 minutes.
3. Reheat the pan and add 1 tablespoon of the oil. Fry the fish for 2 minutes on each side, then remove from the pan and set aside.
4. In a food processor or blender, blend the poppy seeds with their soaking water and another 120ml of water, the mustard seeds, turmeric, coconut, ginger, garlic, green chilli, onion, ground coriander, cumin and chilli powder.
5. Heat the remaining oil in the pan on a medium heat and fry the spice mixture for 6–7 minutes, stirring from time to time and adding a little more water if it becomes too dry. Add 150ml of water and the lemon juice and simmer for 5 minutes.
6. Return the fish to the pan and cook for a further 3 minutes. Serve hot with plain basmati rice.

Bengali Fish – Shorshe Jhol

Mustard oil is extracted from pressed mustard seeds; it is dark yellow in colour and slightly pungent. It is often used in east India and Bangladesh and is rich in vitamin E. When buying mustard oil, do make sure it's the type suitable for cooking and internal use. As an alternative to white fish, this hot and spicy recipe can also be made with an oily fish such as sardines.

PREPARATION TIME: 5 MINUTES
COOKING TIME: 15 MINUTES
SERVES 4

750g white fish fillets, such as cod, haddock or pollack
½ tsp turmeric
3 tbsp mustard powder, such as Colman's
¼ tsp chilli powder
¼ tsp salt (optional)
3 tbsp mustard oil
¼ tsp nigella seeds
2 green chillies, chopped at an angle

1 Sprinkle the fish pieces with the turmeric and set aside.
2 Mix the mustard powder, chilli powder and salt, if using, with about 6–8 tablespoons of water to make a thick paste. Set aside.
3 Heat a pan on a medium heat and add 2 tablespoons of the oil. Carefully add the fish pieces and fry for 2–3 minutes on each side. Remove from the pan and set aside.
4 Add the remaining 1 tablespoon of oil to the pan on the heat. Add a few of the nigella seeds; when they start to crackle, tip in the remaining seeds and sauté for a minute. Add the mustard paste and cook for 2 minutes.
5 Add the chillies, mix well and cook on a low heat for 2–3 minutes.
6 Return the fish to the pan, mix carefully and simmer for a couple of minutes. Serve hot with plain basmati rice.

Mackerel in Red Chilli – Bangda aur Lal Mirch

Oily fish such as mackerel are a rich source of omega-3 essential fatty acids and also have high levels of potassium, so if there's one food that's good for your heart, it's oily fish. This dish is flavoured with a hot and spicy mix of red and green chillies.

PREPARATION TIME: 10 MINUTES
COOKING TIME: 15 MINUTES
SERVES 2-3

2 mackerel, cut across into 4–5 steaks
½ tsp turmeric
¼ tsp salt (optional)
2 tbsp rice flour
2 tbsp olive oil
3–4 dried red chillies
½ tsp cumin seeds
1 tsp coriander seeds
5–6 black peppercorns
1 tsp tamarind concentrate
4 garlic cloves
1 onion, roughly chopped
1 tsp peeled and grated fresh root ginger
2 green chillies, chopped

1 Place the mackerel on a plate and sprinkle over the turmeric and salt, if using. Sprinkle over the rice flour and coat the fish in the flour.
2 Heat a frying pan on a medium heat and add 1 tablespoon of the oil. Put the fish in the pan and fry for 5–6 minutes, turning once. It will become slightly crunchy and reddish brown. Remove from the pan and set aside.
3 Place the red chillies, cumin and coriander seeds, peppercorns, tamarind, garlic and onion into a blender and blend to a coarse paste.
4 Heat the remaining 1 tablespoon of oil in the pan. Add the fish and the spice mixture and cook for a couple of minutes. Pour in about 2 tablespoons of water to make a slightly runnier sauce.
5 Add the ginger and green chillies, mix and cook for a further minute. Serve hot with chapatis.

Salmon with Chilli and Garlic

Salmon is an oily fish that's high in omega-3, an essential fatty acid that may reduce the risk of some cancers, high blood pressure and heart disease.

PREPARATION TIME: 5 MINUTES
COOKING TIME: 20–30 MINUTES
SERVES 4

4 salmon steaks, approximately 175–200g each
a few washed and chopped coriander leaves

For the marinade
4 garlic cloves, crushed
2 tbsp olive oil
½ tsp chilli powder
½ tsp turmeric
2 tsp lemon juice
¼ tsp freshly ground black pepper
¼ tsp salt (optional)

1 Preheat the oven to 180°C/gas mark 4.
2 Line a baking tray with a sheet of foil, allowing plenty of foil to wrap around the salmon steaks.
3 Mix together all the ingredients for the marinade in a small bowl.
4 Place the salmon steaks in the baking tray and pour half of the marinade over the steaks. Turn the steaks over and pour the rest of the marinade over the other side.
5 Loosely cover the steaks with the foil and bake in the centre of the oven for 20–30 minutes until cooked.
6 Sprinkle over the coriander leaves and serve hot.
7 You can slip off the skin with a knife before serving.

Keralan Dry Sautéed Coconut Prawns

Prawns are a low-fat source of protein and are a healthy choice for a main meal. Coconut is quite high in saturated fat, so should be considered an occasional treat. The combination of coconut with seafood is a match made in food heaven and is especially popular in southern India.

PREPARATION TIME: 10 MINUTES, PLUS 10 MINUTES MARINATING
COOKING TIME: 20 MINUTES
SERVES 4

¼ tsp turmeric
¼ tsp chilli powder
¼ tsp salt (optional)
400g peeled, cooked small prawns
3–4 garlic cloves, crushed
1 tsp peeled and grated fresh root ginger
1 green chilli, finely chopped
2 tbsp groundnut oil
6–8 curry leaves, finely chopped
1 onion, finely chopped
2 tsp ground coriander
100g fresh or frozen grated coconut
½ tsp tamarind concentrate

1 Mix the turmeric, chilli powder and salt, if using, in a bowl large enough to hold the prawns. Add the prawns and mix well. Then add the garlic, ginger and green chilli and stir into the prawns. Cover and place in the fridge for 10 minutes.
2 Heat the oil in a saucepan on a medium heat and add the curry leaves, then add the onion and sauté for 5–6 minutes until lightly browned.
3 Add the ground coriander and stir for a minute, then add the coconut and sauté for 3–4 minutes until lightly browned.
4 Add the prawns and their marinade and cook for 5–7 minutes until well combined. Serve hot with plain basmati rice.

Spicy Prawns – Jhinga Masala

Prawns, like other shellfish and fish, are a good source of omega-3 fatty acids. Although they are a low-fat source of protein, prawns can be high in sodium and so should be eaten in moderation. Asafoetida is the dried resin of a gum tree, often sold in powdered form. It is commonly used in Indian cooking, added in minute quantities, and is said to aid digestion; it is often added to lentil and pulse dishes.

PREPARATION TIME: 10 MINUTES
COOKING TIME: 15 MINUTES
SERVES 4

2 tbsp sunflower or olive oil
1 onion, finely chopped
6 garlic cloves, crushed
2 green chillies, chopped
500g large raw prawns, shelled
pinch of asafoetida
¼ tsp chilli powder
1 tsp ground cumin
1 tsp turmeric
200ml light coconut milk

1 Heat the oil in a large saucepan on a medium heat. Add the onion, garlic and green chillies and fry for 2 minutes until the onion is translucent.
2 Add the prawns and stir-fry for another 2 minutes. Remove from the heat.
3 In a small bowl, mix together the asafoetida, chilli powder, cumin and turmeric. Add this mixture to the prawns and stir for a minute. Add 250ml of just-boiled water and simmer for 2 minutes.
4 Add the coconut milk and simmer for another 5–6 minutes. Serve hot with plain basmati rice and a mixed vegetable curry.

CHAPTER 7

Lamb

Indian Muslims are expert in preparing lamb dishes, although the most commonly eaten red meat in India is goat. A balanced diet can include red meat such as lamb, which is a fairly good source of iron. The type of meat you choose and how it is cooked can make a considerable difference to the amount of saturated fat it contains. In general, opt for leaner cuts. The lamb dishes in this chapter should be eaten in moderation, with vegetables on the side.

Cardamom Karahi Lamb

Cardamom stimulates the digestive system and is a good remedy for travel sickness. It is also believed to possess anti-depressant properties and is used in both sweet and savoury Indian dishes such as this luxurious lamb dish.

PREPARATION TIME: 10 MINUTES, PLUS 1 HOUR MARINATING
COOKING TIME: 30 MINUTES
SERVES 4

1 tbsp tomato purée
175ml natural yogurt
1 tsp garam masala
2 tsp peeled and grated fresh root ginger
4–6 garlic cloves, crushed
¼ tsp chilli powder
¼ tsp salt (optional)
225g lean boneless lamb, cut into strips
3 tbsp olive oil
2 onions, finely sliced
6–8 green cardamoms
2.5cm piece of cinnamon stick
a few washed and chopped coriander leaves

1 Mix the tomato purée, yogurt, garam masala, ginger, garlic, chilli powder and salt, if using, in a bowl large enough to hold the lamb.

2 Put the lamb pieces in the bowl and mix. Cover and leave to marinate in the fridge for about an hour.

3 Heat 2 tablespoons of the oil in a pan, add the onions and fry for 5–7 minutes until lightly browned. Remove the onions from the pan and leave them to cool.

4 Place the onions in a food processor and whizz them into a thick purée.

5 Heat a large frying pan on a medium heat and add the cardamoms. Toss them for about 30 seconds until you can smell the aroma. Tip them on to a plate and leave to cool. When they are cold, grind them to a medium to fine powder in a pestle and mortar or a spice mill.

6 Add the remaining 1 tablespoon of oil to the frying pan. When the oil is hot, add the cinnamon, then add the onion purée and the lamb and mix in the ground cardamom. Fry for about 2 minutes.

7 Cover and reduce the heat and cook, stirring from time to time, until the meat is cooked through. If it looks dry, add about 150ml of water.

8 Garnish with the coriander leaves and serve hot with chapatis.

Lamb Kolhapuri – Kolhapuri Lamb Masala

A spicy dish from Maharashtra in western India. Instead of the Kolhapuri spice blend you could use a ready-made medium hot curry powder, but bear in mind that some commercial blends contain salt.

PREPARATION TIME: 15 MINUTES
COOKING TIME: 40 MINUTES
SERVES 4

500g lamb leg steaks, cut into 2cm pieces
4 garlic cloves, crushed
¼ tsp tamarind concentrate
¼ tsp salt (optional)
½ tsp turmeric
2 tbsp groundnut or sunflower oil
2 tbsp Kolhapuri spice blend (page 12)
125ml light coconut milk

1 Put the lamb on a plate and add half of the garlic, the tamarind, salt (if using) and turmeric. Coat the lamb with the spices and set aside.
2 Heat the oil in a pan, add the remaining garlic and sauté for a minute. Then add the Kolhapuri spice blend and mix.
3 Add the marinated lamb and cook, stirring, for 2–3 minutes until the lamb turns brown. Add about 250ml of water and simmer for 30–35 minutes until the lamb is tender.
4 Stir in the coconut milk and simmer for a minute. Serve hot with plain basmati rice.

Spiced Minced Lamb with Black Olives

Although olives are not an ingredient traditionally used in Indian cooking, more and more people in India are exploring different flavours and combining them with spices. In this recipe, olives get the curry treatment. They are rich in iron but do contain a considerable amount of sodium.

PREPARATION TIME: 10 MINUTES
COOKING TIME: 25 MINUTES
SERVES 4

3 tbsp olive oil
1 onion, chopped
4–6 garlic cloves, chopped
2 green chillies, chopped
500g lean minced lamb
1 tbsp tomato purée
1 tsp ground cumin
1 tsp ground coriander
½ tsp turmeric
¼ tsp chilli powder
¼ tsp garam masala
2 tsp peeled and grated fresh root ginger
12–15 black pitted olives

1   Heat 2 tablespoons of the oil in a saucepan or wok on a medium heat. Add the onion, garlic and chillies and fry for a minute.
2   Add the minced lamb and fry for 8–10 minutes until the mince is nicely browned.
3   In a small bowl, mix the tomato purée with the remaining 1 tablespoon of oil, the cumin, coriander, turmeric, chilli powder and garam masala to form a thick paste. Add to the lamb and cook for a further 8–10 minutes.
4   Add the ginger and stir, then add the olives and mix well.
5   Serve hot with chapatis.

Lamb Meatballs in Tomato Curry – Keema Kofta

The word *kofta* is a Persian word which is now used in India, Central Asia and the Middle East through to the Balkans and North Africa. Koftas are generally meatballs, although there are vegetarian koftas too. This recipe uses lean minced lamb but you could make an even lighter dish by using minced skinless chicken.

PREPARATION TIME: 10 MINUTES
COOKING TIME: 35-40 MINUTES
SERVES 4-6

500g lean minced lamb
1 tsp garam masala
2 green chillies, finely chopped
handful of washed and chopped coriander leaves

For the sauce
3 tbsp sunflower or olive oil
2 onions, finely chopped
2 tsp peeled and grated fresh root ginger
4–6 garlic cloves, crushed
½ tsp turmeric
1 tbsp ground coriander
¼ tsp ground cumin
¼ tsp chilli powder
200g tomatoes, washed and chopped
¼ tsp salt (optional)
¼ tsp garam masala

1   To make the meatballs, put the lamb, garam masala, green chillies and coriander leaves in a bowl and mix well. Roll into golf-ball-sized pieces and set aside or cover and place in the fridge.
2   To make the sauce, heat a large pan on a medium heat and add the oil, then add the onions and fry for 7–8 minutes until lightly golden.
3   Add the ginger and garlic and fry for 2 minutes.
4   Add the turmeric, ground coriander, cumin and chilli powder and mix well for a minute.
5   Add the tomatoes and cook on a low heat for 2 minutes until droplets of oil appear on the surface. Add 300ml of just-boiled water and stir well.
6   Now put the meatballs into the sauce and stir in the salt, if using. Cook for 15–20 minutes.
7   Sprinkle over the garam masala and serve hot with plain basmati rice.

Northern Indian Lamb Curry – Old Delhi Nihari

Ginger is among the healthiest and most flavourful ingredients in Indian cuisine. Among its health benefits, it is used to assist digestion, curb nausea and combat the symptoms of colds and flu. When combined with a little cinnamon, it has also been found to reduce muscle pain and stiffness in joints.

PREPARATION TIME: 15 MINUTES
COOKING TIME: 55 MINUTES
SERVES 4

1 tbsp sunflower oil
2 bay leaves
4 cloves
2 green cardamoms
2cm piece of cinnamon stick
600g lean boneless lamb, cut into 2cm pieces
½ tsp chilli powder
½ tsp ground coriander
½ tsp turmeric
1 tbsp natural yogurt
1 tsp peeled and grated fresh root ginger
3–4 garlic cloves, crushed

For the spice masala
1 tbsp fennel seeds
¼ tsp black peppercorns
¼ tsp cumin seeds

To garnish
1 onion, sliced and lightly fried
2 green chillies, cut into strips
3cm piece of fresh root ginger, peeled and cut into thin strips
a few washed and chopped coriander leaves

1 First make the spice masala. Heat a pan on a medium heat and add the fennel seeds, peppercorns and cumin seeds and toast for a couple of minutes. Leave to cool and then grind to a medium to fine powder in a spice mill or a pestle and mortar.

2 Heat the oil in a pan on a medium heat and add the bay leaves, cloves, cardamoms and cinnamon. Add the lamb and fry for 2–3 minutes.

3 Add the chilli powder, ground coriander, turmeric and yogurt followed by the ginger and garlic and cook on a low heat for 15–20 minutes until droplets of oil appear on the surface.

4 Add the spice masala to the pan of lamb and cook for a minute.

5 Pour in 500ml of just-boiled water and cook on a low heat for 20–25 minutes until the lamb is tender.

6 Garnish with the fried onion, green chillies, ginger and coriander leaves.

Lamb Chops Curry – Changezi Champ

Cashew nuts are a good source of several essential minerals such as magnesium and trace elements such as copper, which keeps your immune system healthy and helps the body absorb iron. Like most other nuts, they are also high in healthy fats, which help you feel fuller after a meal.

PREPARATION TIME: 10 MINUTES, PLUS 30 MINUTES MARINATING
COOKING TIME: 25 MINUTES
SERVES 4

8 lamb chops
2 tsp peeled and grated fresh root ginger
4 garlic cloves, crushed
¼ tsp salt (optional)
2 tsp lemon juice
10–15 unsalted cashew nuts
2 tbsp olive oil
1 tsp ground white pepper
½ tsp chilli powder
4 tbsp single cream
¼ tsp garam masala

1   In a bowl large enough to hold the lamb chops, mix the ginger, garlic, salt (if using) and lemon juice together. Add the lamb chops and coat them with the mixture. Cover and place in the fridge for 30 minutes.
2   Grind the cashew nuts in a pestle and mortar or a spice mill and set aside.
3   Heat a large frying pan on a medium heat and add the oil. Add the lamb chops with the marinade and cook until browned on both sides; this should take around 12–15 minutes.
4   Add the white pepper and chilli powder and mix well. Then add 300ml of just-boiled water and cook on a low heat for 8–10 minutes.
5   Stir in the ground cashew nuts and the cream and cook for another minute. Sprinkle over the garam masala. Serve with runner beans.

CHAPTER 8

Chutneys and Relishes

The word chutney comes from the Hindi word *chatna,* which means to relish or taste. Serving chutneys and relishes as an accompaniment to a meal can tantalise the taste buds and enhance the flavours of the main dishes. Many of India's traditional chutneys and relishes are made from fresh vegetables, fruit and herbs, which are chopped or ground together with a little water, vinegar or lemon juice. Often they are made on the same day that they are eaten. I've included chutneys and relishes that contain small amounts of salt and sugar, but remember that these are intended to be eaten in small quantities: one serving of a chutney or a relish is generally about a tablespoon.

Mint Raita

Mint plays an important role in digestion as the aroma of the herb activates the salivary glands to secrete enzymes that begin the process of digestion. This mint yogurt dip works well with biryani dishes.

PREPARATION TIME: 10 MINUTES
SERVES 4

½ tsp cumin seeds
50g mint, hard stalks removed, leaves washed
30g coriander leaves, washed and roughly chopped
1 green chilli, roughly chopped
¼ tsp caster sugar
pinch of sea salt
pinch of freshly ground black pepper
100ml natural yogurt, whisked

1 Heat a frying pan on a medium heat and add the cumin seeds. Toast them for about 30 seconds until you can smell the aroma of the seeds. Remove from the heat and leave to cool. When cooled, place them in a pestle and mortar and grind to a medium to fine powder.
2 Put the mint leaves and coriander leaves into a blender along with the green chilli, sugar, salt, black pepper and 1 tablespoon of the yogurt and blend to a thick paste.
3 Place the green mixture in a bowl and mix in the remaining yogurt. Chill in the fridge until ready to serve.
4 To serve, sprinkle over the cumin.

Devil's Chutney

This is a sweet and sour chutney that has echoes of Anglo-Indian cuisine from the days of the Raj. The raisins add sweetness to balance the vinegar and the heat of the chilli powder.

PREPARATION TIME: 5 MINUTES
MAKES APPROXIMATELY 10–12 TABLESPOONS

2 onions, roughly chopped
¼ tsp chilli powder
4 tbsp raisins
pinch of salt
2 tbsp malt vinegar

1   Place the ingredients in a food processor and blend together until smooth. If the mixture appears too thick, add a little more vinegar.
2   Serve with a main meal or as a dip.

Gujarati Green Chutney – Hari Chutney

Coriander leaves are widely used as a garnish for Indian dishes but are also found in chutneys and in other dishes. Coriander is high in dietary fibre and is a good source of iron and magnesium, which helps keep bones strong. This chutney is a good way to enjoy the fresh flavours and nutrients of coriander.

PREPARATION TIME: 10 MINUTES
SERVES 4

100g coriander leaves, washed and roughly chopped
50g fresh or frozen grated coconut
4 green chillies, roughly chopped
1½ tbsp lemon juice
1 tsp caster sugar
¼ tsp salt

1   Place all the ingredients in a food processor or blender and whizz to a rough paste.
2   Spoon into a bowl and serve as an accompaniment to a meal.
3   This chutney can be stored in the fridge for up to 3 days. Remove from the fridge 5–10 minutes before serving.

Mum's Coconut Chutney

There are many variations of coconut chutney, but this is my mum's version. Coconut is rich in dietary fibre and healthy fats. It's not meant to be eaten every day but as an occasional treat.

PREPARATION TIME: 5 MINUTES
COOKING TIME: 2 MINUTES FOR TEMPERING
SERVES 4

150g fresh or frozen grated coconut, thawed if frozen
1 green chilli, chopped
small handful of coriander leaves
2 tsp peeled and grated fresh root ginger
¼ tsp salt

For tempering
1 tsp sunflower oil
¼ tsp brown or black mustard seeds
1 dried red chilli
5–6 curry leaves (optional)

1   Place the coconut, green chilli, coriander leaves, ginger and salt in a blender and blend to a medium coarse paste. Put into a non-metallic bowl and set aside.
2   For tempering, heat a small frying pan on a medium heat and add the oil. Add a few mustard seeds; when they start to crackle and sizzle, the oil is ready. Tip in the remaining seeds and the dried red chilli and curry leaves, if using.
3   Carefully pour the tempered mixture over the coconut chutney and serve, or store in the fridge for up to 3 days. Remove from the fridge at least 10 minutes before serving.

Hot and Sweet Shallot Pickle with Mustard Seeds

Shallots contain polyphenolic compounds that are powerful antioxidants. Mustard seeds also contain antioxidants and anti-inflammatory compounds and are good sources of magnesium and selenium, which may help to control blood pressure and relieve migraines.

PREPARATION TIME: 10 MINUTES
COOKING TIME: 15 MINUTES
MAKES APPROXIMATELY 8 TABLESPOONS

4 tbsp olive oil
½ tsp black mustard seeds
10–12 shallots, topped and tailed, peeled and cut into quarters
½ tsp turmeric
1 tsp salt
½ tsp chilli powder
juice of ½ a lemon
2 tbsp demerara or muscovado sugar

1 Heat the oil in a heavy-based saucepan on a medium heat. Add a few mustard seeds; when they begin to crackle, tip in the remaining seeds and stir for 30 seconds.
2 Add the shallots and sauté for 3–4 minutes.
3 Tip in the rest of the ingredients, mix well and continue to cook for 10 minutes.
4 Leave to cool, then place in an airtight jar and store in the fridge for up to 3 days.

Onion and Tomato Chutney – Pyaaz aur Tamatar ki Chutney

Onions are a prized member of the allium family and are closely related to shallots, garlic, leeks and chives. Although they bring tears to our eyes, they are packed with nutrients, many of which are most beneficial when they are eaten raw, as in this chutney.

PREPARATION TIME: 10 MINUTES
COOKING TIME: 7 MINUTES
MAKES APPROXIMATELY 8 TABLESPOONS

2 tbsp sunflower oil
½ tsp brown or black mustard seeds
1 tbsp skinned split black lentils (urad dal) (optional)
2 dried red chillies, coarsely chopped
2 red ripe tomatoes, chopped
2 green chillies, coarsely chopped
¼ tsp salt
2 onions, coarsely chopped

1 Heat a pan on a medium heat and add 1 tablespoon of the oil. Add a few of the mustard seeds; when they start to sizzle, add the remaining seeds followed by the lentils, if using, and dried red chillies. Fry for about a minute until the lentils are golden brown. Tip the mixture into a bowl and set aside.
2 Heat the remaining 1 tablespoon of oil in the pan, then add the tomatoes and green chillies and fry for 5 minutes until the tomatoes are soft and mushy. Mix in the salt. Remove from the heat and leave to cool.
3 Place the lentil and spice mixture in a food processor. Add a little of the cooked tomato mixture and some of the chopped onions and blend to a paste.
4 Add the remaining onion and tomatoes and blend again.

Peanut Chutney

Peanuts are packed with healthy monounsaturated fats and are a good source of protein. Serve this simple relish with a lentil dish and chapatis or rice.

PREPARATION TIME: 5 MINUTES
SERVES 4

100g unsalted roasted peanuts
¼ tsp chilli powder
¼ tsp powdered Himalayan or black salt
1 garlic clove, coarsely chopped

1   Place all the ingredients in a food processor and blend to a paste.
2   Transfer to a container with a lid and store in the fridge for up to 3 days.
3   Remove from the fridge 5 minutes before serving.

Roasted Red Pepper Chutney – Laal Simla Mirch ki Chutney

Red peppers are packed with vitamin C and antioxidants such as beta-carotene and this tasty, vibrant chutney looks good on any dinner table.

PREPARATION TIME: 5 MINUTES
COOKING TIME: 25 MINUTES (IF ROASTING)
SERVES 4

3 red peppers, or a 250g jar of roasted red peppers
2 tbsp olive oil
50g breadcrumbs
50g walnuts, coarsely chopped
½ tsp chill flakes
½ tbsp lemon juice
1 small garlic clove, crushed

1 If using fresh peppers, preheat the oven to 200°C/gas mark 6.
2 Cut the peppers in half, remove the seeds and pith and place them skin side up on a baking tray. Sprinkle over 1 tablespoon of the oil and bake in the oven for 20–25 minutes until the skin is slightly charred.
3 Put the peppers into a bowl, cover with cling film and, once cool enough to handle, peel and discard the skins.
4 Place the roasted peppers in a food processor or blender and add the breadcrumbs, walnuts, chilli flakes, lemon juice, garlic and remaining oil and whizz to a thick paste.
5 Cover and store in the fridge for up to 5 days. Serve chilled.

Tomato Chutney

Tomatoes are a rich source of the phytonutrient lycopene: this is a powerful antioxidant that may protect against heart disease and certain types of cancer. It is easiest for the body to absorb this nutrient from cooked tomatoes rather than raw ones.

PREPARATION TIME: 5 MINUTES
COOKING TIME: 20 MINUTES
MAKES APPROXIMATELY 300G

500g tomatoes
1 tbsp olive oil
¼ tsp nigella seeds
¼ tsp brown or black mustard seeds
¼ tsp ground cumin
¼ tsp chilli powder
½ tsp salt
4 tbsp caster sugar
2 tbsp liquid pectin

1   Using a knife, score an 'X' on the tomatoes and immerse them in a bowl of just-boiled water for 2 minutes. Remove from the water, peel off the skin and discard. Coarsely chop the tomatoes and set aside.
2   Heat the oil in a heavy-based pan on a medium heat. Add a few of the nigella and mustard seeds. When they splutter, add the remaining seeds and stir. Stir in the cumin and chilli powder, then add the tomatoes and cook on a low heat for a couple of minutes.
3   Add the salt, cover the pan and simmer for 5 minutes.
4   Roughly mash the tomatoes. Stir in the sugar and simmer uncovered for 7 minutes.
5   Add the pectin, stir well, then boil the mixture rapidly for 2 minutes until quite thick. Remove from the heat and leave to cool.
6   Spoon the chutney into a sterilised jar with an airtight lid. Store in the fridge for up to 2 months.

CHAPTER 9

Rice and Breads

Carbohydrates are an important part of a balanced diet – although, like anything else, if eaten in excess they will cause weight gain and other health problems. In particular, avoid eating too many carbohydrates at one meal, such as rice and bread, as this is likely to cause blood sugar levels to rise too quickly. Consistently high blood sugar levels can have a negative effect on long-term health. Basmati rice is the variety most often associated with Indian cuisine and it has a lower GI than some other varieties, meaning that it raises blood sugar less rapidly. Flat breads such as chapatis, rotis and naan are a dietary staple in many parts of India. Those made from wholegrain flours are more nutritious, higher in fibre and slower to digest, meaning that they are better for maintaining steady blood sugar levels.

Plain Basmati Rice

Basmati is a long-grain rice; it contains essential amino acids and folic acid and is very low in sodium. However, it is high in carbohydrates so it's generally good to not eat bread with the same meal. Here I've given the absorption method of cooking rice: all the water is absorbed and there should be no need to drain any surplus liquid. The rule to remember when cooking white basmati rice using this method is the ratio of 2:1, which means you use 2 cups of water for 1 cup of rice.

PREPARATION TIME: 2 MINUTES
COOKING TIME: 10-12 MINUTES
SERVES 4

200g white basmati rice

1   Put the rice in a sieve and rinse under cold running water until the water runs clear; this removes any excess starch.
2   Put the rice in a saucepan that has a tight-fitting lid, then pour in 500ml of just-boiled water. Cover the pan and place on a low heat. Leave the rice to simmer for at least 7 minutes before uncovering the pan; the rice should be aromatic – it should not smell burnt.
3   Cover and cook for another 3–4 minutes. The rice is ready when the grains are tender, all the water is absorbed, holes appear on the surface and some of the grains appear to be pointing upwards. Serve piping hot.

Brown Basmati Rice with Garlic

Brown rice is more nutritious and contains more fibre than white rice, but the actual nutrient content depends on the milling processes and how much they have stripped away the layers of bran which contain the wholegrain goodness. This is a deliciously nutty and lemony recipe which works well as an accompaniment to a lentil dish.

PREPARATION TIME: 5 MINUTES
COOKING TIME: 50 MINUTES
SERVES 4

200g wholegrain basmati rice
1 tbsp olive oil
3–4 garlic cloves, finely chopped
1 tbsp lemon juice
a few sprigs of parsley, finely chopped (optional)

1   After rinsing in a sieve with cold water, put the rice in a saucepan that has a tight-fitting lid, pour in 500ml of just-boiled water and bring to the boil.
2   Stir once, cover, and reduce the heat to low. Simmer for 45–50 minutes (do not lift the lid).
3   Remove from the heat and leave to stand, covered, for 5 minutes; then fluff with a fork.
4   Heat a pan on a medium heat and add the oil. Add the garlic and sauté until it begins to change colour (be careful not to overcook the garlic or it will be bitter).
5   Add the rice and sauté for 1–2 minutes.
6   Mix in the lemon juice. Fluff with a fork, and sprinkle with parsley, if using.
7   Serve hot with Tarka Dal (page 92).

Indian Sautéed Rice

This is a great way to spice up leftover rice. When the rice is served, the piece of cassia can be left at the side of the plate. Cooked rice should be reheated only once and served piping hot. If you would like to make this from scratch, 200g of uncooked rice and 500ml of just-boiled water makes enough for 4 people. This dish is good served with natural yogurt.

PREPARATION TIME: 10 MINUTES
COOKING TIME: 10 MINUTES
SERVES 4

3 tbsp sunflower oil
4cm piece of cassia bark or cinnamon stick
½ tsp brown mustard seeds
1 onion, sliced
1 tbsp butter
10–12 unsalted cashew nuts
2 green chillies, chopped
approximately 850g cooked rice
½ tsp turmeric
¼ tsp salt (optional)
¼ tsp garam masala
a few washed and chopped coriander leaves

1 Heat the oil in a wok or a large pan on a medium heat. Add the cassia bark, followed by the mustard seeds, and wait for them to sizzle.
2 Add the onion and fry for 2 minutes until translucent.
3 Add the butter, cashew nuts and green chillies and fry for 2–3 minutes until the cashew nuts turn golden.
4 Add the turmeric and cook for 2 minutes. Then add the cooked rice and carefully fold it into the onion mixture.
5 Mix in the salt, if using, and garam masala and serve hot, garnished with coriander leaves.

Tomato Rice – Tamatar Chawal

The curry bush is native to India and Sri Lanka. The leaves are aromatic with a curry- and citrus-like flavour and a slightly bitter taste. In south India they are used in curries, chutneys and lentil dishes as well as in rice preparations. This recipe fuses flavours of north India with southern spices.

PREPARATION TIME: 15 MINUTES
COOKING TIME: 15 MINUTES
SERVES 4

1 tbsp rapeseed oil
1 tsp brown or black mustard seeds
7–10 curry leaves (optional)
1 onion, chopped
¼ tsp turmeric
¼ tsp chilli powder
¼ tsp salt (optional)
1 tsp tomato purée
200g canned tomatoes, blended
200g white basmati rice

1   Heat the oil in a saucepan on a medium heat and add a few of the mustard seeds; when they crackle, add the remaining seeds, then the curry leaves (if using) and the onion. Fry for 5 minutes until the onion is soft.
2   Add the turmeric, chilli powder and salt, if using.
3   Add the tomato purée and the blended tomatoes and cook for 7–9 minutes until the mixture is quite thick.
4   Add the rice and mix well, then stir in 500ml of just-boiled water. Cover and cook on a low heat for 10–12 minutes until the rice is tender, all the water has been absorbed and some of the rice grains appear to be standing up.
5   Serve piping hot with a lentil dish.

Kashmiri Pulao

This northern Indian rice dish is sweet and spicy. It makes a great accompaniment to a lentil dish with a raita or yogurt-based salad. Raisins and sultanas are a good source of dietary fibre and also contain minerals such as iron, potassium and zinc, which are essential to the body's wellbeing.

PREPARATION TIME: 15 MINUTES
COOKING TIME: 25 MINUTES
SERVES 4

a few saffron strands
1 tbsp milk (optional)
2 tbsp butter or ghee
2 bay leaves
4 cloves
4 green cardamoms
1 large onion, sliced
1 green chilli, chopped
2–3 garlic cloves, crushed, or 1 tsp garlic paste
1 tsp peeled and grated fresh root ginger, or 1 tsp ginger paste
10–12 sultanas or raisins
15–20 unsalted cashew nuts
10 almonds
¼ tsp salt (optional)
200g white basmati rice, rinsed

1 In a small bowl, soak the saffron strands in milk or warm water and set aside.
2 Heat the butter or ghee on a medium heat in a saucepan that has a tight-fitting lid. Add the bay leaves, cloves and cardamoms and stir, making sure they do not burn.
3 Add the onion and fry for 5–7 minutes until golden brown.
4 Add the chilli and fry for a minute. Then mix in the garlic and ginger and tip in the sultanas or raisins, cashew nuts, almonds and salt, if using.
5 Stir in the rice and mix well, then add the saffron liquid and pour in 500ml of just-boiled water.
6 Reduce the heat to low, cover with the lid and leave to simmer for 7–9 minutes. Do not lift the lid for at least 7 minutes.
7 The rice is ready when the grains are tender, all the liquid is absorbed, holes appear on the surface and some of the grains appear to be pointing upwards. Serve piping hot.

Vegetable Biryani

This recipe recreates one of India's most popular dishes using brown instead of white rice. Brown basmati rice is less processed than white basmati, so it retains more of its wholegrain goodness. Brown basmati is rich in fibre and helps in maintaining a healthy body weight. It is also a good source of some B vitamins and various essential minerals.

PREPARATION TIME: 25 MINUTES, PLUS 20 MINUTES SOAKING
COOKING TIME: 1 HOUR
SERVES 4

200g brown basmati rice, rinsed
4 tbsp olive oil
½ tsp cumin seeds or shahi jeera (black cumin seeds)
1 tbsp peeled and grated fresh root ginger
5–6 garlic cloves, crushed
500g frozen mixed vegetables (such as cauliflower florets, carrots and green beans)
2 tbsp fresh mint leaves, finely chopped
2 tbsp coriander leaves, chopped
2 green chillies, slit lengthways
1 tsp garam masala or 2 tbsp biryani paste
4 tbsp natural yogurt, whisked
8–10 saffron strands
2 tbsp milk
2cm piece of cinnamon stick or cassia bark
3–4 cloves
4–5 green cardamoms
3 black cardamoms
10 unsalted cashew nuts, coarsely crushed
20 almonds, roughly chopped or coarsely crushed

1 Soak the rice in water for 20 minutes.
2 Heat 3 tablespoons of the oil in a large pan, add the cumin seeds and sauté for a few seconds. Then add the ginger and garlic and stir for a minute.
3 Add the vegetables and stir-fry for 3 minutes.
4 Add 1 tablespoon of the mint and 1 tablespoon of the coriander leaves and the green chillies, then add the garam masala or biryani paste and cook for 2 minutes.
5 Mix in 2 tablespoons of yogurt and cook for about 5 minutes. Remove from the heat and set aside.
6 Place the saffron and milk in a small bowl and set aside.
7 Drain the rice. Heat a large saucepan and add the remaining 1 tablespoon of oil. Tip in the cinnamon, cloves and cardamoms. Add the drained rice and mix well, then stir in 500ml of just-boiled water. Cover and cook on a low heat for 45 minutes. Drain any excess water.
8 Preheat the oven to 180°C/gas mark 4.
9 Place half of the vegetable mixture in a casserole dish, then add the remaining 2 tablespoons of yogurt and the cashew nuts and almonds, stir to mix.
10 Tip in half the rice. Add the remaining vegetable mixture and cover with the remaining rice.
11 Add the remaining coriander and mint leaves. Sprinkle over the saffron and milk. Cover the dish and place in the oven for 15–20 minutes until the rice is cooked. Serve hot.

Peas Pulao

Basmati rice is traditionally used throughout northern India. If you buy rice in a packet, be sure to follow the instructions; if you buy it in bulk or from an Asian shop, it's advisable to rinse it well.

PREPARATION TIME: 5 MINUTES
COOKING TIME: 20 MINUTES
SERVES 4

200g white or brown basmati rice
1 tbsp groundnut oil
2 bay leaves
5–6 cloves
2 x 5cm pieces of cinnamon stick
4 green cardamoms
¼ tsp turmeric
1 dried red chilli
¼ tsp salt (optional)
150g frozen peas or petit pois, defrosted
sprigs of mint, to garnish

1   Put the rice in a sieve and rinse under cold running water until the water runs clear. Leave to drain.
2   In a heavy-based pan with a tight-fitting lid, heat the oil on a low heat and add the bay leaves, cloves, cinnamon, cardamoms, turmeric and dried red chilli, and fry for 30 seconds.
3   Tip in the peas and sauté for 3 minutes.
4   Add the rice and mix well, then pour in 500ml of just-boiled water, cover and cook for 12–14 minutes until the rice is tender. Serve piping hot.

Unleavened Breads – Chapatis

Indian unleavened breads are known as chapatis, rotis or phulkas and are made from a flour known as *atta*, which is milled from hard (durum) wheat. Hard wheats have a high gluten content, which provides elasticity and robustness to the dough, so it can be rolled out quite thin. The traditional chapati is made from stoneground wholewheat and is roasted on a pan (or in an oven). This type of Indian bread contains plenty of complex carbohydrates for sustained energy, and fibre to keep you feeling full for longer.

PREPARATION TIME: 15 MINUTES
COOKING TIME: 15 MINUTES
MAKES 5-6

200g wholewheat flour or atta (chapati flour), plus extra
   for dusting
1 tsp sunflower or olive oil

1 Put the flour in a large bowl and add the oil. Stir in enough tepid water to make a soft dough – about 125ml. Knead for 10 minutes until the dough is elastic; it should not be sticky.
2 Break off golf-ball-sized pieces of dough and roll these out on a floured surface to form circles about 15cm in diameter. As you roll, dust each chapati with a little flour, to prevent it from sticking and to allow the rolling pin to move freely.
3 Heat a heavy-based frying pan or griddle on a medium heat.
4 Place a circle of dough in the pan and cook for 20 seconds on one side, then turn it over and wait until bubbles appear on the surface.
5 Turn it over again and cook the first side.
6 Using the back of a tablespoon, press firmly around the edge so the chapati puffs up. Repeat with the remaining dough. Serve immediately.

Carom Flatbreads – Ajwain Paratha

In the Western world, the seeds of ajwain or ajowan (also known as carom or bishop's weed) are just beginning to emerge as a spice to be reckoned with. In Ayurvedic medicine, ajwain seeds are used to treat stomach aches and indigestion as well as flu symptoms.

PREPARATION TIME: 10 MINUTES
COOKING TIME: 15 MINUTES
MAKES 8

300g wholewheat flour or atta (chapati flour), plus extra
   for dusting
1 tsp olive or sunflower oil
1 tsp carom (ajwain, ajowan) seeds
120g natural yogurt
a little butter, melted (optional)

1. Sift the flour into a large bowl, tipping in the bran left in the sieve. Make a well in the centre and add the oil and the carom seeds to the well.
2. Gradually add the yogurt and stir until the mixture forms a soft dough. Add about 1–2 tablespoons of water if the dough is dry and does not come together.
3. Knead the dough for about 7–9 minutes until it is soft and elastic.
4. Divide the dough into 8 pieces of roughly equal size. Shape each piece into a ball and dust with a little flour to prevent them from sticking, then roll them out on a lightly floured surface to form circles about 15cm in diameter.
5. Heat a heavy-based frying pan on a medium heat until a splash of water sizzles on the surface.
6. Place a circle of dough in the pan and cook for 20 seconds or until the surface starts to darken. Using tongs, turn the paratha over and continue cooking for about 30 seconds until bubbles appear on the surface.
7. Flip the paratha over again and use the back of a tablespoon to press firmly around the edge of the paratha so it puffs up slightly.
8. Remove the paratha from the pan and put it on a clean tea towel; brush with a little butter, if using, then wrap it in the towel to keep warm while you cook the remaining parathas one at a time. Serve warm.

Yeast Breads – Khameeri Roti

Many Indian breads are made from *atta*, a flour milled from hard wheat varieties that are high in protein, thus making the dough more elastic and robust.

PREPARATION TIME: 30 MINUTES, PLUS 45 MINUTES RESTING
COOKING TIME: 5 MINUTES
MAKES 8

1½ tsp fresh yeast
400g wholewheat flour or atta (**chapati flour**), plus extra
   for dusting
butter or ghee for greasing the baking tray

1 Dissolve the yeast in 120ml of tepid water and set aside.
2 Place the flour in a large bowl and make a well in the centre. Add about 240ml of tepid water and gradually mix into the flour, kneading to make a firm dough. Leave the dough to rest for 15 minutes.
3 Then sprinkle the dissolved yeast liquid over the dough. Knead again until the dough is smooth and elastic, without any cracks; it should not be sticky.
4 Cover the dough with a damp cloth to prevent it from drying out and set aside for 30 minutes.
5 Preheat the oven to 180°C/gas mark 4. Grease a baking tray and line with baking parchment.
6 Divide the dough into 8 pieces and shape into balls. Dust each ball with flour and roll each one out to form a circle about 20cm in diameter.
7 Place the discs on the lined tray and bake in the oven for 4–5 minutes until they've risen slightly and turned golden. Serve hot with a lamb curry.

CHAPTER 10

Salads

A serving of salad is the ideal way to increase the nutritional value of your meals. I'd go so far as to say you can never have too much salad – although bear in mind that you can have too much dressing if it contains oil, salt or sugar. Avoid adding too much salt to your salads; instead, highlight the flavours with lemon or lime juice, vinegar or a pinch of freshly ground black pepper. Vary the vegetables you use in order to get a good range of different nutrients. Salads are low in carbohydrates and are a great way to boost the fibre content of light meals. However, if you're not used to eating salad with every meal, start by adding small amounts and gradually increase the quantity.

Carrot Salad

PREPARATION TIME: 15 MINUTES
COOKING TIME: 7 MINUTES
SERVES 4

4 tsp coconut oil
1 onion, finely chopped
1 tsp peeled and grated fresh root ginger
1 green chilli, finely chopped
200g carrots, peeled and grated
1 tsp brown or black mustard seeds
2 dried red chillies, broken in half

1   Heat a pan on a medium heat, add 3 teaspoons of the oil, then add the onion and sauté for 4–5 minutes until translucent.
2   Add the ginger and fry for another minute, and then add the green chilli, stir in the carrots and sauté for a further 2 minutes.
3   Remove the pan from the heat and tip the mixture into a bowl.
4   In the same frying pan, add the remaining teaspoon of oil and then tip in the mustard seeds. When they start to crackle, add the red chillies and mix. Pour the mixture over the salad and serve.

Crunchy Potato Salad – Aloo Chaat

PREPARATION TIME: 10 MINUTES
COOKING TIME: 30 MINUTES
SERVES 4

800g baby or new potatoes, such as Charlotte
1 tsp sunflower oil
1 tbsp unsalted butter
1 tsp ground coriander
1 tsp ground cumin
½ green chilli, finely chopped
1 tbsp washed and chopped coriander leaves
4 spring onions, finely chopped
½ tsp chaat masala (page 6)
½ cucumber, finely sliced
3 tbsp mango chutney
juice of ½ a lemon

1   Bring a large pan of salted water to the boil and cook the potatoes for 15–20 minutes until just tender. Drain and set aside.
2   Meanwhile, heat the oil and butter in a large frying pan, then add the ground coriander, cumin and chilli and cook for 2–3 minutes until fragrant.
3   Add the potatoes and crush them gently to flatten. Cook on a medium to high heat for 5 minutes, turning once, until golden and crisp.
4   Once the potatoes are cooked, stir through the coriander and spring onions and mix well. Sprinkle with the chaat masala and then mix in the cucumber.
5   Combine the mango chutney and lemon juice together in a bowl and drizzle over the salad.

Cucumber Salad

Cucumber makes a refreshing salad; alternatively, substitute with a courgette, washed and sliced.

PREPARATION TIME: 5 MINUTES
SERVES 4

1 cucumber, sliced or chopped
3 tomatoes, chopped
½ red onion, chopped
2 tbsp olive oil
1 tbsp balsamic vinegar
¼ tsp coarsely ground black pepper

1 Place the cucumber, tomatoes and onion in a large bowl.
2 Drizzle with olive oil and balsamic vinegar. Add the black pepper and serve immediately.

Keralan Red Onion Salad

Red onions are a good source of the flavonoid known as quercetin, which can help to reduce the risk of stroke and coronary heart disease if eaten as part of a balanced diet. Eating the onions raw increases the amount of quercetin your body can absorb. This salad from southern India is a quick and simple 'pickle' with vinegar and lemon juice. If you find the flavour too strong, you could add a peeled and grated carrot to give the salad a sweeter taste.

PREPARATION TIME: 10 MINUTES
SERVES 4

1 tbsp malt vinegar
juice of 1 lemon
2 green chillies, finely chopped
¼ tsp salt (optional)
pinch of freshly ground black pepper
3 red onions, thinly sliced

1 Mix the vinegar, lemon juice, green chillies, salt, if using, and pepper together in a non-metallic bowl.
2 Add the onions and mix well. Serve within a few hours.

Pomegranate Yogurt Salad – Anardana ka Raita

PREPARATION TIME: 10 MINUTES
COOKING TIME: 5 MINUTES
SERVES 4

500ml natural yogurt, whisked
pinch of salt
pinch of coarsely ground black pepper
seeds from 1 pomegranate
1 tbsp sunflower oil
½ tsp cumin seeds
a few washed and chopped coriander leaves

1 Place the yogurt in a bowl, mix in the salt and pepper and fold in the pomegranate seeds.
2 Heat a frying pan on a medium heat and add the oil. Add a few of the cumin seeds; when they start to crackle, add the remaining seeds and fry for about 20 seconds. Make sure the seeds do not burn.
3 Carefully pour the mixture on to the yogurt and garnish with the coriander leaves.
4 Serve chilled with a rice dish such as a biryani.

White Radish Salad – Mooli ka Salaad

Radish is a good source of dietary fibre and also contains vitamin C. White radishes are also known as mooli or daikon and are extremely popular in Indian cuisine; they are used in curries and breads. But to reap the full nutritional benefits, try them in a salad such as this one, combined with a little chilli and tomato.

PREPARATION TIME: 15 MINUTES
SERVES 4

1 white radish, peeled and grated
1 tsp peeled and grated fresh root ginger
1 tomato, finely chopped
1 green chilli, finely chopped
2 tsp lemon or lime juice
a few washed and chopped coriander leaves

1 Place the radish, ginger, tomato and green chilli in a non-metallic bowl and mix together. Sprinkle over the lemon or lime juice.
2 Garnish with the coriander leaves just before serving.

CHAPTER 11

Drinks

Apart from water, drinks are not generally served alongside meals in India; from a health point of view it's certainly a good idea to avoid sweetened fizzy drinks and juices. The long hot summers make ice-cold drinks a necessity rather than a luxury and Indians enjoy a variety of drinks, from cool and fragrant to hot and spicy. The herbs and spices used in Indian drinks are intended to have either a heating or cooling effect on the body and often meant to stimulate the mind.

India is a nation of tea drinkers and grows some of the world's finest teas, such as Assam. The delicate flavours of these aromatic leaves make a refreshing infusion to enjoy at any time of day. If you usually add sugar to your tea, try to cut back gradually by using a little less each week; your taste buds will adapt and you'll be able to fully appreciate the flavours of your tea. In this chapter, I've included my version of Masala Chai (page 193), using a typical combination of spices.

Cumin Cooler – Jal Jeera

Cumin stimulates the digestive system and may help in removing toxins from the body. This is a spicy detox tonic which is generally drunk in the summer months. Black salt is used in many Indian dishes; it is an Indian rock salt that becomes pinkish grey in colour when ground. As well as sodium it contains other minerals, which give it its savoury sour flavour.

PREPARATION TIME: 10 MINUTES
SERVES 4

10–12 washed and coarsely chopped mint leaves
a few washed and coarsely chopped coriander leaves
½ tsp peeled and grated fresh root ginger
2 tsp cumin seeds, roasted and ground
½ tsp black salt
1 tsp mango powder (amchur)
1 tsp caster sugar
4 lemon slices and 4 sprigs of mint, to garnish

1 Put the mint and coriander leaves and ginger in a blender and blend to a fine paste.
2 Add 1 litre of chilled water, the cumin, black salt, mango powder and sugar and stir.
3 Strain and serve chilled, garnished with a slice of lemon and mint.

Dates Shake – Khajoor ka Shake

Dates are a good source of various vitamins and minerals, such as selenium, copper and magnesium, which means they can help to strengthen bones and reduce the risk of conditions such as osteoporosis. This shake also includes bone-building calcium from the milk, combined with the natural sweetness of dates.

PREPARATION TIME: 7 MINUTES
SERVES 4

4–5 dates, stoned or pitted
500ml semi-skimmed or almond milk
seeds from 2–3 green cardamoms, ground

1 Chop the dates into small pieces.
2 Put the dates with the milk and cardamom into a blender and blend until smooth.
3 Pour into 4 glasses and serve.

Apple and Ginger Zinger

For centuries ginger has been known for its medicinal properties and in particular for its ability to combat nausea and ease digestion. In addition it's believed to improve the brain's focus and sharpen memory. The compounds that produce its health-promoting properties are also what give fresh ginger root its delicious hot and spicy zing.

PREPARATION TIME: 8 MINUTES
SERVES 4

600ml apple juice
2 tsp peeled and grated fresh root ginger
juice of 1 lime
¼ tsp coarsely ground black pepper
500ml sparkling water
4 sticks of lemongrass

1   Pour the apple juice into a jug.
2   Put the ginger in a tea strainer, place over the jug and press with the back of a teaspoon to squeeze out as much of the ginger juice as possible. Put the leftover ginger pulp into the apple juice.
3   Stir in the lime juice and the black pepper. Leave to infuse for a couple of minutes, or cover and leave in the fridge for up to 3 hours.
4   Strain the mixture into a large jug.
5   Just before serving, pour in the sparkling water. Pour into 4 glasses and serve with a stick of lemongrass.

Homemade Lemonade – Nimbu Paani

Nimbu paani is an Indian version of lemonade, which can be made either sweet or salty. Cardamom has an intense and floral flavour that lends itself to both sweet and savoury dishes. This spice may help to alleviate digestive problems such as heartburn, constipation and intestinal gas.

PREPARATION TIME: 5 MINUTES
SERVES 4

juice of 1 lemon
4–5 green cardamoms, slightly crushed
2 sprigs of mint, washed
2 tsp runny honey
750ml sparkling or still water

1   Mix all the ingredients together in a large jug, stirring to ensure the honey has dissolved.
2   Serve chilled or with ice cubes.

For an intense cardamom flavour, remove the seeds from the cardamoms and crush them thoroughly. Mix into the water and then strain the mixture before serving.

Orange and Saffron Flame

Being hydrated improves one's mood and having something a little different from plain drinking water makes a welcome change. In this recipe, the water is infused with the most expensive spice in the world. Saffron is the dried stigmas of the flower of *Crocus sativus*; these are painstakingly handpicked and then each strand is laid out to dry. Saffron has been found to ease depression and some studies have indicated that it may be useful in treating Parkinson's disease and other age-related degenerative conditions.

PREPARATION TIME: 7 MINUTES
SERVES 4

400ml sparkling or still water
100ml orange juice
4 tsp peeled and grated fresh root ginger
10–12 saffron strands
seeds from 4–6 green cardamoms, crushed
cinnamon stick for stirring

1 Mix the water and orange juice in a jug.
2 Put the ginger in a tea strainer, place over the jug and press with the back of a teaspoon to squeeze out as much of the ginger juice as possible. Discard the fibrous pulp.
3 Add the saffron and the cardamom seeds and stir well with the cinnamon stick. Pour into 4 glasses and serve.

Turmeric Milk – Haldi Doodh

Turmeric milk, known for its anti-bacterial and anti-viral effects, is used to treat colds and flu or as a hot tonic. My mother gives me this remedy when I'm feeling a little under the weather with the sniffles. You can use ground or dried sliced turmeric, or fresh turmeric root.

COOKING TIME: 5 MINUTES
SERVES 1

250ml semi-skimmed or full cream milk
1 tsp turmeric
1 tsp runny honey (optional)

1 Place the milk in a saucepan and bring to the boil. Add the turmeric, stir and leave to infuse for a minute.
2 Strain into a cup and mix in the honey, if using. Serve hot and sip a little at a time.

Vanilla Lassi

Lassis are commonly made in the summer with a tart dairy product such as buttermilk or yogurt and are often lightly spiced or flavoured with seasonal fruits such as mangoes. For this version, I've used vanilla extract, which adds a sweet and gently spicy note.

PREPARATION TIME: 5 MINUTES
SERVES 4

600ml milk
600ml natural yogurt
2 tsp vanilla extract

1 Place all the ingredients in a bowl or a jug. Using a hand-held blender or a balloon whisk, mix all the ingredients together until well combined.
2 Serve chilled or with ice cubes.

Indian Almond Milk – Basundi

Generally this rich drink is made with butter and cream. I've turned it into a healthier treat that can be drunk hot in the winter and cold during the summer months. I've used evaporated milk for a creamy beverage minus the sugar.

PREPARATION TIME: 7 MINUTES
COOKING TIME: 5 MINUTES
SERVES 4

400ml evaporated milk
seeds from 4 green cardamoms, ground
8–10 saffron strands
1 tbsp ground almonds
6 pistachio nuts, chopped

1   Pour the evaporated milk into a small saucepan and heat gently for 3 minutes.
2   Add the cardamom seeds, saffron, almonds and pistachios and stir for 2 minutes.
3   Serve in small shot glasses, hot or chilled.

Hot Lemon Water

According to Ayurveda, the ancient Indian practice of traditional medicine, drinking a cup of warm lemon water every morning gives a long-lasting boost of energy, encourages healthy digestion and reduces bloating. Lemons are a rich source of potassium and vitamin C. I've added a little honey to soften the flavour.

PREPARATION TIME: 3 MINUTES
SERVES 1

250ml water, freshly boiled
1 tsp lemon juice
½ tsp runny honey

1 Pour the warm water into a heatproof glass.
2 Stir in the lemon juice and honey. Sip a little at a time.

Indian Spiced Tea – Masala Chai

Black tea has strong antioxidant properties, which counteract the damaging effects of free radicals (molecules that form in the body, particularly as a result of exposure to the sun and to pollution). A cup of masala chai makes a great pick-me-up packed with powerful spices.

PREPARATION TIME: 5 MINUTES
COOKING TIME: 7 MINUTES
SERVES 2

2cm piece of cassia bark or cinnamon stick
1 green cardamom, slightly crushed
2 cloves
2.5cm piece of fresh root ginger, peeled and crushed, or ¼ tsp ground ginger
¼ tsp fennel seeds
2 tsp loose Assam tea
125ml full cream or semi-skimmed milk

1 Bring about 375ml of water to the boil in a saucepan and then add all the spices and continue boiling for a couple of minutes.
2 Take the pan off the heat and tip in the tea. Reduce the heat to low, put the pan back on the heat and simmer for 1 minute.
3 Add the milk and continue to simmer for a further 2 minutes.
4 Strain the tea into small cups and serve at once.

Kashmiri Tea – Kahwa

Cloves, cinnamon, ginger and cardamom mixed with green tea can relieve headaches and it is a comforting way to maintain fluid levels.

PREPARATION TIME: 5 MINUTES
COOKING TIME: 10 MINUTES
SERVES 4

2 green cardamoms, crushed
2cm piece of cinnamon stick
2.5cm piece of fresh root ginger, peeled and sliced
2 cloves
4 tsp green tea leaves
4 pinches of saffron strands
8 almonds, blanched, skinned and chopped
2 tsp caster sugar (optional)

1   Bring 750ml of water to the boil in a saucepan and then add the cardamoms, cinnamon, ginger and cloves. Leave to infuse for a few seconds and then add the tea leaves and turn the heat down to a gentle simmer.
2   Soak the saffron in a tablespoon of warm water and set aside.
3   Strain the tea into a jug. Add the saffron water and the almonds, and the sugar, if using, and stir to dissolve the sugar. Serve hot.

CHAPTER 12

Desserts

In India 'desserts' are eaten around teatime or during festivals and not every day, so limit your intake of Indian sweets such as *jilebis* (Indian-style doughnuts) and *barfi* (Indian fudges) to special occasions. Instead of eating a pudding after a meal, opt for a piece of fresh fruit or a few dried fruits, such as raisins, apricots and cranberries. Although many Indians have a sweet tooth, I've reduced the amount of sugar in most recipes in this chapter.

Almond and Apricot Bites – Badaam aur Jardaloo ki Barfi

Dried fruits are high in dietary fibre but are also high in sugar, because their natural sugars are concentrated when they are dried. These give a good energy burst before exercising.

PREPARATION TIME: 10 MINUTES, PLUS 30 MINUTES FREEZING
MAKES 25 PIECES

140g almonds
150g raisins
½ tsp ground cinnamon
10 dried apricots, chopped
50g unsweetened desiccated coconut

1 Place the almonds, raisins and cinnamon in a food processor and blend into a smooth, thick paste; this should take about 3 minutes.
2 Add the apricots and pulse for 30 seconds, and then add the coconut and pulse for another 10 seconds.
3 Remove the mixture and place it on a large piece of cling film. Pull up the cling film on either side and press it together to form a square about 4cm thick, keeping the layer of cling film between your hands and the mixture to prevent sticking.
4 Wrap up the square and place it in the freezer for 20–30 minutes. This will make it easier to cut.
5 Using a sharp knife, cut the square into 25 smaller squares.

Almond Rice Dessert – Badaam Phirni

This is a rich ground rice pudding that is made for special occasions and festivals. I've reduced the amount of sugar considerably, leaving just enough to enhance the rose flavour. Almonds are high in healthy fats, so although that makes them high in calories, a few almonds consumed as a snack reduces hunger pangs.

PREPARATION TIME: 10 MINUTES, PLUS 3 HOURS SOAKING
COOKING TIME: 15 MINUTES
SERVES 4

2 tbsp white basmati rice
500ml semi-skimmed milk
3 tbsp caster sugar
seeds from 2–3 green cardamoms, crushed
1 tsp rose water or 2–4 drops of rose extract
18–20 almonds, blanched and chopped

1 Soak the rice in 6 tablespoons of water for 3 hours.
2 Drain the water. Put the rice into a blender along with 2 tablespoons of water and grind to a smooth paste.
3 Pour the milk into a non-stick saucepan on a medium heat. Add the ground rice, sugar and crushed cardamom seeds and cook for about 10 minutes, stirring constantly to prevent the mixture from sticking, until it is thick.
4 Remove from the heat and stir in the rose water or extract. Transfer to a serving bowl, cover and place in the fridge to chill.
5 Serve cold. Add the almonds before serving.

Apple Halwa

This can be served cold, or warm during the winter months. It can also be used as the base for a spiced apple oat crumble. Peel the apples just before cooking them to avoid discoloration.

PREPARATION TIME: 20 MINUTES
COOKING TIME: 20 MINUTES
SERVES 6

2 tbsp ghee or unsalted butter
1kg apples (weight before peeling), peeled, cored and chopped
¼ tsp ground cinnamon
1 tsp vanilla extract
2 tbsp caster sugar
3 tbsp ground almonds

1   Heat a pan or a wok on a medium heat and add the ghee or butter.
2   Tip in the apple pieces and sauté for 10–15 minutes until the apples are soft. Mash them and continue sautéing until the mixture becomes quite thick.
3   Add the cinnamon, vanilla and sugar and stir. Add the almonds and mix well for 2 minutes. Continue to stir and cook until the mixture starts to come away from the sides of the pan.
4   Remove from the heat and serve warm, or leave to cool, then cut into squares or shape into balls.
5   Apple halwa can be covered and stored in the fridge for 3–4 days.

Cranberry Granola Kulfi

The two main ingredients in granola are oats and nuts, which makes it a nutritious and filling food – although it can contain quite a lot of sugar or honey. I've added it to an Indian ice cream recipe, with cranberries and additional nuts for a delicious treat.

**PREPARATION TIME: 10 MINUTES,
PLUS AT LEAST 6 HOURS FREEZING
COOKING TIME: 10 MINUTES
SERVES 4**

200ml semi-skimmed milk
a few saffron strands
2 tbsp dried cranberries
1 tbsp runny honey
2 tbsp double cream
3–4 almonds, chopped
4–6 pistachio nuts, chopped
2 tbsp granola or any crunchy muesli cereal

1 Pour the milk into a saucepan and bring to the boil.
2 Add the saffron, cranberries and honey and stir well for a minute. Then stir in the cream, nuts and granola.
3 Remove from the heat and leave to cool slightly.
4 Pour the mixture into ice lolly or kulfi moulds, or a freezerproof container with a lid and freeze for at least 6 hours, or ideally overnight, until the ice cream has set.
5 Take the kulfi out of the freezer 10–15 minutes before serving to allow it to soften slightly.
6 Serve one small scoop per person or one ice lolly mould per person.

Dry Fruit Halwa

Dried fruits are high in calories because their natural sugars are concentrated when they are dried. Even so, sugar is sometimes added, so read the label to check before buying. Although this is a high-calorie dessert, it is also high in dietary fibre and healthy fats, so a small amount will keep you feeling full.

PREPARATION TIME: 10 MINUTES
COOKING TIME: 8 MINUTES
SERVES 4

2 tbsp walnuts, slightly crushed
20 almonds, slightly crushed
2 tbsp unsalted cashew nuts, broken or slightly crushed
2 tbsp unsweetened desiccated coconut
1 tbsp ghee or unsalted butter
seeds from 5–6 green cardamoms, finely crushed
2 tbsp dried tropical fruit such as pineapple and papaya pieces
2 tbsp sultanas and raisins
5–6 stoned dates, chopped
pinch of grated nutmeg

1   Heat a pan on a medium heat and add the walnuts, almonds and cashews. Toast them for a couple of minutes, then tip on to a plate and set aside.
2   Then tip the desiccated coconut into the pan and toast for a minute. Add to the plate with the nuts.
3   Add the ghee or butter to the pan and when melted, add 60ml of water. Mix well and then stir in the cardamom and cook until the mixture is bubbling.
4   Add all the dried fruits, the nutmeg and the toasted nuts and mix well. Cook on a low heat for a few minutes until the mixture starts to come away from the sides of the pan.
5   Serve warm in small bowls with a dollop of crème fraîche or single cream.

Eastern Fruit Salad

Mango is often known as the king of fruits. Although ripe mangoes are rich in sugar, they are also rich in vitamin C and are a good source of vitamin A and many health-protecting antioxidants; among other benefits they are believed to improve the skin. Papayas are also packed with vitamins A and C. This is an indulgent fruit salad to enjoy as an occasional treat.

PREPARATION TIME: 20 MINUTES, PLUS CHILLING
SERVES 4

1 papaya, washed
1 ripe mango, washed
2 kiwi fruits, peeled and sliced
handful of strawberries, washed and hulled
1 banana, sliced
2 tsp lime juice
¼ tsp ground cardamom
2 tsp demerara or muscovado sugar (optional)

1 Peel the papaya with a knife, then cut it lengthways, scoop out and discard the seeds and cut the flesh into 2.5cm pieces.
2 Slice the mango lengthways either side of the large flat stone. Place the two sides flesh side up and make criss-cross cuts into the flesh without cutting through the skin. Push the skin up gently to make the cubes stand out, then cut away the cubes of flesh.
3 Put the papaya and mango into a bowl and add all the remaining ingredients. Stir gently to combine. Cover the bowl with cling film and put in the fridge for about 30 minutes.
4 Remove from the fridge a few minutes before serving to take off the chill. Divide between 4 bowls and serve.

Fruit Salad with Spiced Syrup

Most fruits are naturally low in sodium and fat and are a good source of vitamins and minerals, especially vitamins A and C, plus potassium and folic acid. Star anise not only imparts a liquorice-like flavour and a delightful fragrance but also includes antioxidants and is believed to aid digestion.

PREPARATION TIME: 15 MINUTES, PLUS 25 MINUTES CHILLING
COOKING TIME: 5 MINUTES
SERVES 4

1 large mango, peeled and chopped
1 large pink grapefruit, peeled and chopped
4 small oranges, peeled and segmented
seeds from 1 large pomegranate

For the syrup
the juice of 2 oranges or 50ml orange juice
2 tbsp agave nectar or runny honey
2 star anise
¼ tsp ground cinnamon

1 Place the mango, grapefruit and orange segments in a bowl and mix gently. Cover with cling film and place in the fridge to chill for 20 minutes.
2 Meanwhile, place all the ingredients for the syrup in a saucepan and warm through over a low heat for 2–3 minutes. Mix well, then remove from the heat and leave to cool.
3 When cold, cover and chill in the fridge for 20 minutes.
4 Just before serving, divide the fruits between 4 bowls. Drizzle over the syrup and sprinkle with the pomegranate seeds. Serve immediately.

Carrot and Cardamom Pudding – Gaajar ka Halwa

Carrots contain a host of vitamins and minerals; many of their health benefits can be attributed to their high beta-carotene and fibre content. Beta-carotene is a powerful antioxidant that the body converts into vitamin A; it plays a vital role in the health of our eyes and skin. This indulgent pudding is traditionally made with plenty of full fat milk and sugar but this is a lighter version, with the added dimension of the two spices.

PREPARATION TIME: 10 MINUTES
COOKING TIME: 40 MINUTES
SERVES 6-8

1 tsp butter
350g carrots, peeled and finely grated
410g can reduced-fat evaporated milk
2 tsp caster sugar
seeds from 6–8 green cardamoms, ground
pinch of saffron
1 tbsp sultanas (optional)
1 tbsp ground almonds

1   Put the butter in a large saucepan and add the carrots. Cook, stirring, for 2 minutes, then add the evaporated milk and cook, partly covered, on a low to medium heat, for about 30 minutes until the milk has been absorbed.
2   Stir in the sugar using a wooden spoon and cook for a few minutes more, adding a tiny drop of sunflower oil if you feel that the mixture is sticking to the bottom of the pan.
3   Add the cardamom and saffron and mix well. Stir in the sultanas, if using, and the ground almonds.
4   Serve hot or cold, in small bowls.

Indian Apricot Whip – Khubani ka Meetha

Dried apricots are excellent sources of dietary fibre and are high in potassium, which is essential for maintaining healthy blood pressure. This sweet dish from Hyderabad is served on special occasions. It is usually made with cream but here I have used yogurt instead.

PREPARATION TIME: 20 MINUTES
SERVES 4

500ml natural yogurt
2 tsp runny honey
juice of ½ a lemon
125g soft dried apricots, coarsely chopped
2 tbsp chopped nuts, such as almonds or walnuts

1 Place the yogurt in a bowl and whisk in the honey. Continue stirring while you add the lemon juice.
2 Fold in the apricots and stir in the nuts. Cover and place in the fridge for 15 minutes before serving.

Indian Lemon Mousse – Nimbu ka Shrikhand

Lemons are available all year round and in Indian cuisine are used mainly in savoury dishes. Choose a large juicy lemon for this recipe. This divine dessert is the Indian version of a mousse, but it's not made with eggs.

PREPARATION TIME: 5 MINUTES, PLUS 8 HOURS DRAINING
SERVES 4–5

450g natural yogurt
4–5 saffron strands
1 tbsp milk
4 tsp caster sugar
2 tsp lemon juice
pinch of grated nutmeg
1 tbsp single cream
grated zest of 1 lemon

1   Put the yogurt in a large piece of muslin cloth. Tie the ends of the cloth and attach it to a fork or a knife and suspend the cloth over a bowl to collect the liquid. Place in the fridge for about 8 hours or overnight.
2   Put the saffron and milk into a cup and leave to soak for a couple of minutes.
3   In a bowl, whisk together the sugar, lemon juice and nutmeg.
4   Carefully open the muslin bundle and put the strained yogurt into the bowl with the sugar and lemon juice, discarding the liquid. Whisk together, adding the cream while whisking. The mixture will stiffen.
5   Stir in the saffron milk. The saffron will give the dessert a light yellow gold colour. Fold in the lemon zest and chill before serving.

Cardamom and Cinnamon Cookies

In Ayurveda, cinnamon is classed as a 'warming' spice. Among other things, it is believed to help regulate blood sugar: increased blood sugar levels can cause excess fat to be stored, especially round the stomach area. This is a less sugary version of India's famous biscuits known as *nan khatai*.

PREPARATION TIME: 10 MINUTES
COOKING TIME: 15 MINUTES
MAKES APPROXIMATELY 24 BISCUITS

80g unsalted butter, softened
60g caster or demerara sugar
1 tsp vanilla extract
seeds from 4–6 green cardamoms
150g wholemeal flour
50g fine semolina
½ tsp ground cinnamon

1   Preheat the oven to 180°C/gas mark 4. Line a baking sheet with baking parchment.
2   Cream the butter, then add the sugar and beat until soft and fluffy. Mix in the vanilla extract.
3   Crush the cardamom seeds to a coarse powder and add to the flour and semolina, along with the cinnamon.
4   Add the spiced flour mixture to the butter mixture and knead to form a dough. It will be quite crumbly.
5   Take a piece of the dough and roll into a small ball the size of a ping pong or squash ball. Flatten until about 5mm thick. Alternatively, roll out the dough on a floured surface and cut out using a 5–6cm round biscuit cutter.
6   Place the biscuits on the lined baking sheet, spacing them at least 3cm apart. Bake for 12–15 minutes until golden brown.
7   Transfer to a wire rack to cool and harden.
8   Store in an airtight container for up to 3 weeks.

Indian Milk Fudge – Doodh ki Barfi

Barfi is an Indian sweet made from milk that is cooked slowly and reduced to a fudge-like consistency. Milk, including dried milk, is an excellent source of calcium – essential for strong bones – and B vitamins, which have many vital roles in maintaining good health.

PREPARATION TIME: 5 MINUTES, PLUS COOLING
COOKING TIME: 10 MINUTES
MAKES 16 PIECES

1 tbsp unsalted butter
2 tsp caster sugar
60ml semi-skimmed milk
seeds from 4–5 green cardamoms, crushed
125g full-fat milk powder

1   Melt the butter in a heavy-based saucepan on a medium heat, then add the sugar and cook, stirring continuously, for 3 minutes until the sugar has dissolved.
2   Add the milk and the cardamom and simmer, stirring occasionally, for 2–3 minutes.
3   Tip in the milk powder and continue to simmer, stirring, for 5 minutes or until the mixture becomes stiff and begins to come away from the sides of the pan.
4   Turn the mixture out on to a sheet of greaseproof paper and leave it to stand for a couple of minutes, then use a wet palette knife or spatula to shape into a 10cm square about 3.5cm thick. Leave to cool completely.
5   Using a sharp knife, cut the cooled fudge into sixteen 2.5cm squares.
6   Serve immediately with coffee, or transfer to an airtight container and store in the fridge for up to 5 days.

Pistachio and Almond Indian Fudge – Pista Badaam Barfi

Barfi is a popular Indian sweetmeat, found in many different varieties. This version is flavoured with pistachios and almonds, rich in vitamin E and B vitamins.

PREPARATION TIME: 5 MINUTES, PLUS 3 HOURS CHILLING
COOKING TIME: 12 MINUTES
MAKES APPROXIMATELY 16 PIECES

20 shelled pistachio nuts
10 almonds
1 tbsp unsalted butter
2 tsp caster sugar
60ml semi-skimmed milk
½ tsp cardamom seeds, crushed (seeds from 4–5 green cardamoms)
1 tsp rose water (optional)
5–6 saffron strands
125g full-fat milk powder

1 Heat a frying pan on a medium heat, add the pistachios and almonds and gently toss for 2 minutes, then leave to cool. Crush the nuts using a pestle and mortar until they are coarsely ground.

2 Melt the butter in a heavy-based saucepan on a medium heat, then add the sugar and cook, stirring continuously, for 3 minutes.

3 Add the milk and simmer for 3 minutes, then add the cardamom, rose water, if using, and the saffron. Mix well.

4 Tip in the milk powder and continue to simmer, stirring, for 3 minutes.

5 Tip in the crushed nuts and stir for 2 minutes or until the mixture becomes stiff and begins to come away from the sides of the pan.

6 Turn the mixture out on to a sheet of greaseproof paper and shape into a 10cm square, about 3.5cm thick.

7 Cover and place in the fridge for 3 hours, then cut into 2.5cm squares or diamonds.

8 Store in an airtight container in the fridge for up to a week. Remove from the fridge 10 minutes before serving.

Indian Orange Fudge – Narangi Barfi

Nagpur in western India is famous for its oranges, which are often used to flavour regional sweetmeats such as this delicious zesty orange fudge. Orange zest is the outer layer of the orange's peel. It contains the fruit's oils, and adds flavour to a variety of dishes.

PREPARATION TIME: 15 MINUTES, PLUS COOLING
COOKING TIME: 15 MINUTES
MAKES APPROXIMATELY 24 PIECES

2 oranges
125g unsalted butter
150g plain flour
50g caster sugar
125g full-fat milk powder

1 Wash the oranges thoroughly. Grate the zest and set aside. Then peel the oranges, removing as much of the white pith as possible. Coarsely chop the flesh, then place it in a blender and whizz to a medium-coarse purée.
2 Heat a non-stick saucepan on a medium heat and add the butter. Tip in the flour and, using a wooden spoon, mix well for 2–3 minutes until the flour turns golden brown.
3 Mix in the orange zest, then gradually stir in the orange purée.
4 Stir in the sugar and the milk powder and cook for 5–7 minutes until the mixture is thick and comes away from the sides of the pan.
5 Tip it on to a greased baking tray, approximately 20cm square, and leave to cool completely.
6 Once set, cut the fudge into small squares. Serve at room temperature.
7 Store in an airtight container in the fridge for up to 3 days.

Acknowledgements

A huge thank you to mum Kami for putting up with all my recipe testing and thank you to Meno, Candice, Isla, Eva, Jasmyn, Alice, David, Nikki Read, Giles Lewis, Amanda Keats, Maggie Ramsay, Open Age's Helen Leech, Jenny Marshall and Russell John, Taz Virdee, Will Halfacree, Spice Drops Gouri Kubair, Littlepod Janet Sawyer, Tosh Verma, Sharan Verma, Sunita Verma, Frances Ma, Saryu Mehta, Monir Ali, Abha and Bill Adams, Tanya d'Alcor, Barry Quinn, Helen Hokin, Roberta Vaitkute, Pauline Barrett, Robin Barrett, Liat Barrett, Neil McLeod, Jonathan Sommers, Shika Patel and Emilie Malik.

Index